THE
CHAOS
IMPERATIVE

ALSO BY ORI BRAFMAN

Click: The Magic of Instant Connections (with Rom Brafman)

Sway: The Irresistible Pull of Irrational Behavior (with Rom Brafman)

The Starfish and the Spider: The Unstoppable Power of Leaderless Organizations (with Rod A. Beckstrom)

THE
CHAOS
IMPERATIVE

(How Chance and
Disruption Increase
Innovation, Effectiveness,
and Success)

ORI BRAFMAN
and *Judah Pollack*

CROWN
BUSINESS

NEW YORK

Copyright © 2013 by Shechinah Inc.

All rights reserved.

Published in the United States by Crown Business, an imprint of the Crown Publishing Group, a division of Random House, Inc., New York.

www.crownpublishing.com

CROWN BUSINESS is a trademark and CROWN and the Rising Sun colophon are registered trademarks of Random House, Inc.

Crown Business books are available at special discounts for bulk purchases for sales promotions or corporate use. Special editions, including personalized covers, excerpts of existing books, or books with corporate logos, can be created in large quantities for special needs. For more information, contact Premium Sales at (212) 572-2232 or e-mail specialmarkets@randomhouse.com.

Library of Congress Cataloging-in-Publication Data
Brafman, Ori.
    The chaos imperative / Ori Brafman and Judah Pollack.
        pages cm
1. Organizational effectiveness. 2. Chaotic behavior in systems. I. Pollack, Judah. II. Title.
HD58.9.B7333 2013
658.4'01—dc23   2013016803

ISBN 978-0-307-88667-5
eISBN 978-0-307-88669-9

Printed in the United States of America

Jacket design by Base Art Co.

10 9 8 7 6 5 4 3 2 1

First Edition

To Hilary Roberts,

who brings order to the chaos

Contents

INTRODUCTION

The Bottom Line

Ron Ricci at Cisco Systems claims there are two types of communicators in life: the up-front, bottom-line crew, and the people who like to tell a good story and provide you with the evidence before arriving at their thesis. Ron refers to the two groups as "deductive communicators" and "inductive communicators," respectively. I am an inductive communicator, I've come to realize. I typically hate jumping straight to the bottom line. Especially in a book about chaos, of all things. I much prefer making my case with a good story.

But for all you deductive communicators out there, here is the bottom line, up front: we all need what I call contained chaos in our lives and careers. We can gain immeasurably from conducting a meeting with absolutely no agenda or from bringing unusual suspects into the fold. My research has shown that a certain amount of chaos supports what I call "organized serendipity"— where new and creative ideas seem to emerge out of nowhere.

Surprisingly, chaos makes us *more* effective in our careers. It makes for better school systems, more innovative businesses, and, as my work with the U.S. Army has shown, even a more resilient military.

So that's the bottom line. Now let me tell you a story.

(I)

HARNESSING CHAOS

Make It Matter

I was sitting in an office with General Martin Dempsey months before he became the chairman of the Joint Chiefs of Staff. He wanted to know if I could help him.

In his late fifties, with close-cropped white hair and wearing his combat uniform, Dempsey certainly looked the part of a top military officer. But as I began talking to him, he didn't exactly fit the stereotype I had in my mind. He's affable, well versed in literature and the classics, soft-spoken, down-to-earth, and quick to smile.

I met General Dempsey in his office at Fort Monroe, Virginia. It was a long, rectangular room in which every wall was decorated with plaques, ceremonial swords, and photos taken on the battlefield.

Three days earlier, I had been sitting on a Northern California lawn overlooking an organic garden, wearing shorts and flip-flops, and talking to my San Francisco friends about the importance of "setting a vibe" at a music camp-out (where several hundred people take to the woods, hauling a bunch of speakers and power sources with them, and DJs spin in the forest).

Now here I was, still a little sunburned, on a military base on the East Coast. There was nothing touchy-feely about the swords hanging on the wall. The steel was sharp, spotless, and very real. I felt more than a little out of place. My only prior exposure to the military had come from watching Hollywood's war movies and from seeing soldiers carrying Uzis when I was a young kid in Israel, before my family moved to the United States. (My father was such a poor fit for the Israeli military that he was assigned to a kibbutz for his compulsory service and spent his time harvesting bananas.) I majored in peace and conflict studies at the University of California at Berkeley. I live in San Francisco and I'm a vegan.

Walking to General Dempsey's office that morning, I'd realized that I didn't know any of the proper etiquette. Do you salute a general? (You don't if you're a civilian.) Do you call him "sir"? (I called him Marty.) Do you monitor your language? (I didn't, and neither did he.) I hadn't even known what the four stars on a general's uniform meant—I'd had to look it up on Wikipedia.

We sat across from each other on comfortable brown leather couches. It was an informal meeting, but just a few feet away, seven members of his uniformed staff were taking copious notes. It was as if a team of highly trained soldiers—ready to respond to any situation or surprise attack—were documenting your visit to your uncle's house.

"I was on a trip," he told me, "reading your first book, *The Starfish and the Spider*, and I immediately turned to one of my officers and said that I really wanted to meet you, because I think you can help me with something very important." I'd later learn that as I was living my life in San Francisco, people in the highest echelons of the Pentagon were using my theories to try to understand how to counter terrorism and how to dramatically change the nature of the military. But more on that in a bit.

As Dempsey and I talked about his time as one of the top commanders in charge of the Iraq war, I noticed a rectangular wooden box about the size of a shoebox on the coffee table between us. There was something about it that captured my attention: it was simple but carefully constructed, and it was one of the only objects in the room that was closed. I asked him what was inside. It turned out that the box's contents represented the reason he was asking for my help.

He opened the box and pulled out what looked like baseball cards. But instead of a picture of an athlete, each card bore a photo of a soldier in uniform. "These are all the soldiers," Dempsey told me, "who died in action under my command." The inscription on the box stated simply, *Make It Matter*. Dempsey still keeps in touch with the soldiers' families. As he handed me card after card, it seemed as if they collectively represented the weight of his responsibilities.

Dempsey was rather beloved by the troops. He wasn't your usual hard-nosed, the-world-is-the-way-that-I-see-it autocrat. Earlier in his career he'd been an English professor at West Point, and his students remember his special fondness for Shakespeare. When he served in Iraq, his division was ready to go home after a long tour of duty and was literally at the Kuwaiti border when, at the last minute, it was ordered to stay another few months to take part in the attack on Fallujah, which would turn out to be one of the most difficult and bloodiest battles of the Iraq war. Dempsey is famous for the speech he gave to inform his troops that although they had done their duty, they were not going home yet:

instead of sugar-coating the news, he was honest in ac-
knowledging just how difficult the war had been.

Like many of us, I'd always assumed military leaders
were unfailingly supportive of our nation's foreign en-
gagements and conflicts. But Dempsey's tone, like that of
many top military leaders I've since encountered, was
much more nuanced and reflective. As he handed me
one card after another, each with a young face on it, he
talked about how he did not want to add more cards to
that box.

He told me he recognized that the army was too rigid
in its ways, too concerned with bureaucracy as opposed
to effectiveness. It was so mired in paperwork that new
ideas and innovation had no chance to take root. The
institutional army was known on the inside as a place
where good ideas went to die.

"Ori," he said, "how do I change the army?"

The military, like most of our other major institutions,
has waged a century-long campaign to become more
efficient. It has created more sophisticated weapons,
lowered casualty rates, and built supply lines from California to Afghanistan. A variation on this same quest
for efficiency and productivity has seeped into our companies and our personal lives as well. We eliminate waste
and cut production cycle times. We rely on the instant
gratification of emails and texts to communicate with

our colleagues and friends. We mail a package and expect it to be on the other side of the world the next day. We fly thousands of miles in a few hours, yet complain when a plane is delayed by thirty minutes. We've maximized efficiency, but at what cost?

Dempsey was in an especially challenging situation. When I first met him, he was in charge of leadership training in the army, and he soon took the reins of arguably the most powerful organization that's ever existed on earth. But his challenge wasn't *whether* the military should change; it was *how*.

General Dempsey had hundreds of thousands of soldiers under his command. You might think that he could just give an order and his subordinates would jump to execute it. That might be true. But their willingness to execute his orders didn't address Dempsey's real concern—that the army suffered from a lack of imagination, from a lack of innovation. Before 9/11, the army, and for that matter the entire U.S. government and its law enforcement agencies, couldn't imagine the potential scale of destruction from terrorists hijacking airplanes and crashing them into our buildings. Similarly, in preparing for future conflicts, our military is too bounded by previous experience to imagine who or what might be our next enemy or threat. It's not so easy to simply order people to become more imaginative.

Seeing me hesitate, Dempsey asked his question again, in a different way:

"How do we become more adaptive?"

"I'm not sure," I replied candidly. "But I think you need to create more chaos. You need to bring a little bit of the bubonic plague into the army, Marty."

Then I began to tell him a story.

Of Rats and Men

The death toll wasn't measured in mere numbers. It couldn't be: the numbers of the dead were too staggering. It was measured in percentages.

London lost 40 percent of its citizens. Tuscany, 80 percent.

The Black Death arrived with fleas borne on the backs of rats riding the trade ships sailing from Africa and Asia. The plague swept through Europe's medieval cities. It killed farmers and city dwellers alike, and villages became ghost towns. In total, it cut Europe's population nearly in half.

When the plague arrived in 1348, Europe was so poor compared to Asia that the Mongols hadn't even bothered to conquer it. Yet though it was poor, technologically backwards, weakened by drought and crop failures, and with the stench of death in the air, Europe was about to begin its ascent to world dominance. And that rise had everything to do with the death, destruction, upheaval, and disorder that had just befallen it.

The Black Death didn't just have a silver lining. It was actually *instrumental* in bringing about Europe's rise to greatness.

The plague entered Britain through the port of Bristol.

Rats were a common sight in those days, and no one paid attention to one particular rat that scampered down the gangplank and onto the wharf. No one imagined that this six-inch rodent, which happened to play host to infected fleas, would soon wreak so much havoc.

As it scurried through Bristol, it passed some twenty thousand people engaged in trade. Bristol was an inviting place for a hungry rat, which could eat its way through sacks of grain waiting to be loaded onto carts and taken to huge mills. It undoubtedly would have wound its way between barrels of wine from Bordeaux, and perhaps it found a warm bed in bolts of wool cloth waiting for export.

On the busy sidewalks of Corn Street, the rat might have scampered beneath four-foot-tall bronze pillars— known as "the nails"—where merchants struck deals. To the east it would have encountered the thriving ship-building business of the port town. Large piles of timber, sailcloth, and ropes lay about waiting to be assembled into the ships that moved the lifeblood of the city.

It was this busy world of commerce that our infected rat was about to turn upside down. The rat's effectiveness as a vector in spreading the Black Death came as a result of its seeming insignificance. No one would have noticed a rat scampering through the markets, hiding beneath a table in a tavern, or foraging in the pantry of a local nobleman's house. Rats had the run of medieval cities as well as the countryside. A barmaid wearing a skirt exposing a flash of ankle, a cook in the kitchen, even a nobleman—all were vulnerable to the bite of one of the fleas that jumped off our rat's back.

At first there would have been no discernible change. The plague bacteria took two to eight days to incubate. But within a week the infected barmaid would have collapsed to the floor. The cook might have started convulsing, vomiting, or, even more frightening, laughing uncontrollably. The nobleman would have been put to bed, debilitated by the pain shooting through his arms and legs. All of their fevers would have spiked to 105 degrees.

A few days more and swellings the size of an egg would have appeared on the necks, under the arms, or in the groins of the infected individuals. These were known as buboes, thus giving rise to the name *bubonic plague*. The cause of death was often exhaustion, heart failure, or internal bleeding. In all, the death spiral took about ten days.

In addition to infection spread by the bite of a flea, there were two other forms of the infection. One was transmitted via exposure to an infected person's blood; this form killed within a day. The other was airborne and attacked the lungs, causing shortness of breath and a large volume of mucus. This was the kind that most easily passed from person to person. First one by one, then by the thousands, men, women, and children succumbed— not just in Bristol but throughout the continent. In the eyes of medieval Europeans raised on the Book of Revelation, it was the apocalypse.

The plague should have been the end of Europe.

Instead, it brought about a mysterious transformation that has challenged historians: Within 150 years—the blink of an eye in human history—Europeans discovered the New World, invented the printing press, developed oil painting, produced the first eyeglasses, established copyright laws, and, to the exultation of many, distilled the first bottle of whiskey. Soon to follow were other leaps of innovation—Newton's theory of gravity, modern banking systems, and democratic and industrial revolutions.

Europe went from being too insignificant to merit

conquest to experiencing a continent-wide renaissance that would transform it into the most powerful region of the world. The question, of course, is *how*.

The historian David Herlihy writes that the plague "assured that the Middle Ages would be the middle, not the final, phase in Western development." And one of the main reasons for that, he claims, was that "the post-plague period was an age of new men."

The Church Hires Aristotle

While they serve very different purposes and have very different goals, the medieval Church and the modern U.S. Army have a lot in common. Both have hierarchical structures, both operate out of a central headquarters— the Vatican in the former case, the Pentagon in the latter—and both operate on a huge scale. One can even think of the medieval Church as a kind of corporation, with a headquarters, regional offices, and layers of management.

Now imagine the Catholic "corporation" being ravaged by the plague. Prior to the plague, the Church had become weakened by its inability to integrate knowledge from the outside. The Church looked askance at ancient knowledge from the Greeks and Romans, whether it involved philosophy or architecture. It wasn't that no one in the Church was investigating the world. The issue was that lines of inquiry and even reality itself were defined by Church doctrine. If you discovered something in the physical world that defied that doctrine, well then, your fact must be wrong. Thus, though it did not intend to, the Church was stifling progress.

Here is an example of what little regard the Church had for some ancient knowledge. The author Boccaccio describes walking up to the Benedictine monastery in Monte Cassino. Ravaged by the plague, the monastery was half empty. Its library lacked a door, grass was growing inside, and ancient manuscripts, dusty and torn, were piled at random. Shocked, Boccaccio asked what had happened. He was informed that the monks would tear strips of parchment from the manuscripts and sell them as talismans to make money.

Boccaccio tucked under his arms as many of the illuminated manuscripts and parchments as he could and carried them off to preserve them. Boccaccio's love of the ancient manuscripts set him apart from the monks at the monastery. But the monks' disregard for the knowledge contained in those manuscripts isn't surprising. For centuries, few in Western Europe read much from the Romans or the Greeks.

At the time, the Bible was the predominant form of knowledge in Europe, for faith was more important than reason. As St. Anselm said, "I believe that I may understand." This was the dominant paradigm of the Middle Ages in Europe and the source of the Church's power.

Boccaccio was of a different breed, subscribing to the philosophy of the humanists, who, in addition to believing in the importance of the individual, admired the writings of the Greeks and Romans, especially Aristotle and Cicero. However, Aristotle had prescribed a system of rational inquiry, a search for facts, that was at odds with the Church's mandate of faith first. As a result, the Church was hostile to the humanists. While the humanists were scouring old church libraries to scavenge ancient manuscripts and texts, the Church had banned clerics from teaching about Aristotle.

But all that changed with the plague.

At the time of the plague, European society was deeply religious. The Catholic Church played a significant role in every aspect of life, from birth to death. When the plague spread, it was the priests who sat at the bedsides of those who were dying, providing comfort and performing last rites. As a result, the priests had far greater exposure to the pandemic than the rest of the population, and members of the clergy succumbed to the disease at a much higher rate than everyone else. The monastic system, the backbone of the medieval Church, was nearly wiped out by the plague.

The damage to the Church on a spiritual level may

have been even more severe. Once filled with worshippers, churches sat empty during the plague—those individuals who hadn't lost their lives had had their faith tested. If, as they believed, the plague was a punishment sent by God, why were so many members of the clergy dying? People began to believe it was the end of the world, and a bacchanalian mood took over. Former parishioners went to cemeteries to take part in orgies. Prostitutes began to solicit among the gravestones.

But it wasn't just members of the lower classes who were affected. The fact that the plague was so communicable meant it didn't discriminate: wealthy lords and serfs alike succumbed to it. That meant that along with the disease itself, the plague also spread throughout the social strata a loss of religious belief.

Citing the deaths of priests and other religious figures, many members of the nobility who themselves would eventually succumb to the plague cut the Church out of their wills and instead left their money to establish new institutions of higher learning. In the same year that the plague struck in Europe, 1348, the University of Prague was founded. In 1350 the University of Florence was created. Between 1348 and 1372 Cambridge established four new colleges, Oxford two. Universities were established at Vienna, Krakow, and Heidelberg. In these new universities, more people could get an education, and thus more were exposed to the teachings of the humanists.

In fact, the humanists poured into the universities, soon making up much of the faculty as well as the student body. They all fell in love with Aristotle's process of rational inquiry and Cicero's gift for rhetoric.

In other words, the demise of the priests, as tragic as their deaths were, opened up what I call "white space." White space is the first of three elements of chaos that you can harness to increase productivity and innovation in an organization. We're going to take a much closer look at white space later, but for now think of it as a time or place or system unfettered by an established structure. White space is a blank canvas, a new beginning.

For the Catholic Church, white space was created by the lack of clergy. Desperate for new priests, the Church brought in men who previously would have been considered unfit for or unworthy of the priesthood. And this is the second important element of chaos—the openness to bringing in people who are "unusual suspects," outsiders who are not a part of the system. In the case of the Church, the new recruits to the priesthood in the wake of the plague were university graduates who for the most part subscribed to the humanist philosophy. In bringing them into the clergy, the Church unwittingly brought Aristotle into the fold.

Having been educated in the university system, the newly minted clergymen brought with them their admiration for the ancient thinkers, engineers, artists, and architects. The humanists and their presence inside the Church created ripple effects that would last for centuries and eventually usher in the Renaissance.

In 1419 Florence held a competition to see who could complete the dome of the Basilica of St. Mary of the Flowers, which had sat unfinished for over a hundred years. But no one had any idea how to build a freestanding brick dome. The ancient Romans had figured it out, but their writings on architecture had been lost in an age of illiteracy and disregard for scientific knowledge.

In the end, an architect by the name of Filippo Brunelleschi won the contest. He was able to solve the dome problem by studying the Pantheon, the famous Roman dome from antiquity. Brunelleschi examined old texts reclaimed by the humanists. By drawing on knowledge that had been declared off-limits and by inventing new machines to help lift building materials, Brunelleschi succeeded in constructing a giant octagonal brick dome without the aid of so much as a wooden scaffold.

There was an eager young man working in the foundry helping to build some of Brunelleschi's new machines. Fascinated, he often went to the church to watch the machines at work. His name was Leonardo da

Vinci, and he would help to bring the humanists' legacy to succeeding generations.

At the same time, another young man was studying at the University of Florence. The son of a physician, his name was Tommaso Parentucelli, and his studies coincided with the rising influence of the humanists.

He maintained many earthly interests, including architecture, science, history, and literature. As a factotum of the bishop of Bologna and later a diplomatic missionary for the Church, he collected books from wherever the Church sent him. Following his success as a diplomat, he was made a cardinal, and in 1447 he was elected pope—Pope Nicholas V, the first humanist pope.

And what did this humanist pope do? He restored Roman aqueducts and began the construction of St. Peter's Basilica. He oversaw a Church in which a cardinal, Nicholas of Cusa, used reason to invent and craft the first pair of lenses to correct nearsightedness. And he established the Vatican library—to this day one of the world's great repositories of knowledge.

Just a hundred years earlier, the Church had declared nearly everything that was not in the Bible heresy. Now the Vatican was collecting books from antiquity, transcribing them, and protecting them. The Church had undergone a huge cultural shift.

With this shift and the new openness that had arisen

in the white space created by the plague, the Catholic Church in Italy was perfectly positioned to reap the benefits of a colossal shift in global power: the fall of Constantinople. The great Christian city on the Bosporus fell to the Ottoman Turks in 1453.

This should have been a blow to the Church. Constantinople had been a center of learning for hundreds of years. But its Greek citizens fled to the west with their books in their carts, on their backs, and under their arms. When they landed in Italy, these unusual suspects, with their knowledge and their manuscripts, were welcomed and embraced. Pope Nicholas V ordered the Vatican library purchasers to buy their texts en masse to preserve the knowledge within.

This new thirst for knowledge sparked by the humanists brought about a new and overwhelming demand for books. Traditionally, books had been copied by hand. Thousands of monks all over Europe would sit for days on end meticulously copying manuscripts at a rate of two to three pages a day. Before the plague, labor was so plentiful, and therefore so cheap, that this was a viable system.

The plague, of course, killed off many of these monks. The result? No more cheap labor.

At the same time, with the deaths of so many other people, there were mounds of cast-off and discarded clothes. Giant bonfires lit up the sky as these clothes were burned—there weren't enough people to wear them. But soon people began to boil the clothes down into their fibers and make rag paper—lots of rag paper. So while labor was now expensive and scarce, paper was suddenly cheap and plentiful.

By the 1400s there was an interesting confluence of events: a high demand for books, a cheap supply of paper, an economic incentive to create a labor-saving printing device, and a multitude of never-before-seen texts from Constantinople. Along came Johannes Gutenberg and his printing press. Consider the impact of his invention in the context of these factors that helped make it possible: Had it not been for the plague, the humanists would not have come to power and brought with them a surging demand for books. Labor would have remained cheap and paper scarce. In other words, without the plague, there might not have been any need for Gutenberg's press.

One infected rat was all it took. Scurrying through the city, destroying the institutions of the day, it created a ripple felt through nearly every aspect of society—spurring advances in architecture, a church more receptive to science and reason, and even the invention of the printing press—and brought Europe from the dark ages to the Renaissance.

When Chaos Brings Life

After I explained the impact of the plague on Europe, General Dempsey stopped me. "You're suggesting that I make the army more chaotic?"

"Yes," I said.

General Dempsey's surprise was understandable. In our corporations, in other organizations in our communities, and in our personal lives, we strive to minimize chaos, with all its unpredictability and uncertainty. By definition chaos is the enemy of organization. We've sat in meetings where a lack of defined processes has led to interminable wasted hours and negligible results. We've seen the footage of chaos unleashed throughout the world, such as the thousands of homeless people in Haiti after the earthquake. We tend to confront chaos as if it were an unruly beast—something to be contained as much as possible.

Scientists inevitably think of chaos theory and the butterfly effect—how the flapping of the wings of a butterfly in China can lead to a hurricane in the Caribbean. Managers might bolt upright in the middle of the night after a nightmare about chaos on the manufacturing floor that causes the production line to seize up and stop. Parents might recall a particular birthday party at Chuck E. Cheese where the kids ran wild.

Chaos often brings to mind a loss of organization, a

lack of structure, action without a plan, goal, or purpose. The end result tends to be destruction. But what if there's another side to chaos? A benefit—something about chaos that can actually help us be *more* effective? Something in its greater variability, its absence of rigid structure, and its lack of a clear purpose that can lead to revolutionary, as opposed to evolutionary, change?

There is a paradox at the heart of chaos. For all the destructive power of the chaos unleashed by the Black Plague, it turned out to be the crucible in which the modern Western world was forged. We're going to see a similar pattern emerging again and again: Chaos creates white space, which in turn allows unusual suspects to sweep in. The result is a kind of organized serendipity, or what I call contained chaos. It may seem magical and bizarre that the Renaissance came about so quickly after the plague. But we'll see that it was not a random event: the conditions had been created to enable and even ac-celerate serendipity.

Think for a moment of the cliché of a sailor in tat-tered pants sitting alone on a desert isle in the middle of the ocean. He is always sitting beneath a single palm tree. We all know how the sailor got there: he was ship-wrecked. But how did the palm tree get there?

There are about 250,000 different seed-producing plant species in the world, and they have evolved differ-ent ways of transporting themselves to fertile land. Many float through the air. Think of the round, white balls of dandelion seeds that children blow on. The seeds go flying off, catch the wind, and glide to distant pastures. Other seeds stick to the fur of passing animals. Still others wrap themselves in the sweet deliciousness that we call fruit. When animals eat the fruit, the seeds pass through their digestive systems intact and are spread to other parts of the forests and fields.

Of the 250,000 types of seeds in the world, a scant 1 percent of them are able to float in water. Only a quarter of those can survive in the water for more than a week. Even fewer of them can survive in the harsh, salty environment of the open ocean. The coconut is one of these very unusual seeds; in this context it's an unusual suspect. It is nature's oceangoing vessel, capable of surviving for months at sea.

A *high tide* or storm washes the coconut into the sea, where it drifts to and fro on the ocean's waves until it makes landfall. But not just any land will do for a coconut tree to grow. The coconut needs a tropical climate and plenty of rainfall. Most important, it needs open space with lots of sunlight. It cannot grow with a canopy overhead. Like the humanists of the Middle Ages, palm trees need a lot of white space if they are to thrive. That is why there are so many palms along the shoreline. The harsh salt spray prevents most plants and trees from growing, leaving an open space for the coconut to take root and capture the sunlight it needs to grow.

Finally, there is the serendipity of the coconut making landfall. Mother Nature does not release a map of islands that are hospitable to palm trees. The oceans are a matrix of tides, streams, upwellings, and waves, always in motion, and the coconuts follow the currents of the sea. Every time a coconut finds its way to a beach, it is a serendipitous event. But it is not completely random. The ocean's currents create this kind of serendipity over and over again. The process works so well that coconuts have washed up on shore as far afield as Norway and have grown into palm trees from Fiji to the Canary Islands.

In other words, nature is an active proponent of the chaos imperative. The white space of tropical beaches welcomes the unusual suspects of oceangoing coconuts, thanks to the organized serendipity of the ocean currents.

Now imagine if a coconut drifted into Honolulu harbor. A busy harbor is a good metaphor for lots of human organizations. It lacks white space, so no unusual suspects can take root. Every inch of space has been claimed, so there would be nowhere for the coconut to land. This is the situation in many companies. A new idea is suggested, but there is no space for it to land, to take root, to grow into the next new thing.

Or imagine if the ocean had no currents or tides. If the coconut could not travel with the currents, it would just bob in the water, going nowhere. It would never arrive at a new, empty beach where it could grow into a palm tree. This too is true of many organizations. There is no system allowing unusual ideas to flow, to move from one place to another. They just bob in place, never finding a spot to take root and grow.

Or imagine the coconuts had been weeded out and thrown away, as unusual ideas are in many organizations. Lean Six Sigma, efficiency charts, "making your numbers": these are all systems designed to wipe out variance. Out of 250,000 kinds of seeds, why would most corporations bother with the one-quarter of 1 percent that can float in the ocean for months? Why nurture and encourage something so useless and unusual? Yet, given the right context, coconuts are a remarkably creative force.

In fact, nature loves white space and unusual suspects—even if in our eyes they seem chaotic and destructive. Take, for example, sequoia trees, which grow only in the wake of a forest fire. The flames of a forest fire tear through the trees with as much ferocity and as little discrimination as the plague in medieval Europe. Some trees explode from the intense heat. But once the fire has burned out, the forest floor is a white space. The underbrush has been cleared away. Dead wood and plants are transformed into ash and nutrients and absorbed back into the soil. And it is in this environment that sequoia trees can begin to grow. Within a few years or decades, the forest is once again healthy and flourishing, more robust than ever.

Perhaps the most dramatic instance of this paradoxical process, and one linked to the evolution of the human species, is the Chicxulub impact crater in the Yucatán Peninsula.

Have you ever tried rubbing two rocks together to create a spark to start a fire? If you haven't, well, neither have I. If you have, you know that it takes specific conditions to work. One rock needs some iron content, the other flint. But it can be done.

Sixty-five million years ago, that's precisely what happened, on an epic scale. One of the rocks was about ten miles wide. The other rock was the earth. In essence, an asteroid the size of Manhattan was hurtling through space at forty thousand miles per hour when it burned through our atmosphere and struck the earth. The collision ignited a fire that engulfed the entire planet.

When geologists examine the layer of earth from this era, they see a fine, thin line of dust. Below that line they find a wide variety of fossils, from dinosaurs to beetles. Above the line, post-impact—post-chaos—they find almost nothing. The collision wiped out the dinosaurs and nearly every other living thing. So much dust was thrown into the air that it blocked the sun for a long time and the planet's temperature plummeted.

But a few unusual suspects survived, including certain plants, as well as small mammals able to take shelter in caves and under rocks. In this white space—a wide-open ecosystem with few predators—some of these mammals evolved into primates. And of course one of those branched off and evolved into *Homo sapiens*. You are reading this book because organized serendipity and a cosmic act of destruction threw the world into chaos, which gave rise to an explosion of biodiversity tens of millions of years ago.

How Saddam Wins

I've never told Dempsey this, but I don't know whether the army actually does suffer from a lack of imagination. I suspect that it doesn't.

During the days leading up to the 2003 invasion of Iraq, American soldiers were operating in what is known as battle rhythm. Commanding officers and their staffs would work six days a week, fourteen to eighteen hours a day, with only Sunday as a day of rest. But there was one especially workaholic intelligence officer named Steve Rotkoff, a Jewish colonel from New York City.

Rotkoff is an unusual character, not least because there aren't many Jews with strong New York accents in the army. Although fit, Rotkoff doesn't seem like a stereotypical army colonel. This is a man who read all thirty-six of Shakespeare's plays during a single summer break in high school.

Most days Colonel Rotkoff would wake up at 4:30 a.m., be involved in briefings until 11:00 a.m., have till 3:00 p.m. to work on actual in-theater prep, and then spend the hours from 3:00 p.m. to 11:00 p.m. meeting with various Pentagon and intelligence officials.

But on Sundays, Rotkoff and a small group of other officers would get together for open discussion about the army and its mission. "Early on," Rotkoff says, "I realized the need for a little unstructured time to not only bond but to let our minds wander. So I created the Sunday afternoon 'prayer session.'" If you could think imaginatively, you got invited. Rank did not matter. The meeting would last for two to three hours, and there was no agenda. Steve brought pizza and beer.

These meetings were purposely unstructured, to provide plenty of white space for new or unusual ideas. One day a young officer announced that he had a theory he wanted to present to the group. His presentation was entitled "How Saddam Wins." In the presentation, he laid out how Saddam Hussein could empty the prisons, take advantage of the cell-like structure of the Baath Party, make known where all the arms were hidden, and set the Shias and Sunnis at each other's throats as well as ours.

In essence, what the young officer was suggesting was that the U.S. Army wouldn't face the violence of the Iraqi government; it would face the violence of an unshackled and traumatized culture. Saddam's twenty-four-year rule had inflamed tensions inherent in Iraqi culture, and with Saddam out of power, we'd be walking right into the middle of a sectarian blood feud.

Colonel Rotkoff thought the presentation was solid and worthy of consideration. He attempted to get the young officer a meeting with the general staff, but no matter how hard he tried, Rotkoff could not get anyone to listen. Of course, the scenario the young officer sketched out that Sunday is pretty much exactly what happened in Iraq a year later.

My point? The army, like the medieval Church, is a massive bureaucracy with a powerful, entrenched, values-driven culture and a clear sense of purpose. The danger for an organization like this is that it can become too structured. It can eliminate all white space. Unusual suspects are given no voice, and new ideas are stifled. The overhanging canopy of an organization's structure can sometimes block out too much sunlight to allow new ideas to grow.

It was the open-ended format of Steve Rotkoff's Sunday group that left space for the young officer to present his theory. There were few other places in the army's rigid hierarchy for such an idea to emerge so freely.

For new ideas to grow, you also need some unusual suspects. In Steve Rotkoff you had a rare Jewish colonel who thought differently from those around him, as well as a committed group of officers using their day off to think strategically about tactics and ideas they hadn't delved into before.

The third thing you need is what I call organized serendipity. The army did not suffer from a lack of imagination. It suffered from a lack of organized serendipity. The prescient presentation "How Saddam Wins" could not find its way up the chain of command. If it had, the army might well have devised a different strategy; perhaps it would have invaded more cautiously, not rushing headlong to Baghdad but securing areas as it went. Perhaps it would have dropped fewer bombs in the beginning, knowing there was no government to defeat; it might have gone in with vastly more troops and focused on securing peace and making urban areas safe.

That was really General Dempsey's question to me. How can an organization encourage innovative ideas and allow them to move through the system? The answer is that you need to create little pockets of chaos within the larger organization. And that is what *The Chaos Imperative* is all about. In the course of the book I will explore how generals, schoolteachers, business executives, and even video game designers have created pockets of chaos within their established structures and routines in order to foment new ideas and allow them to take hold and grow. I'll examine the three elements of chaos—white space, unusual suspects, and organized serendipity—and show how they can be consciously created. But first I need to define what I mean by the word *chaos* and explore how to go about creating pockets of chaos within an existing organization.

(2)

CONTAINED CHAOS

When we were growing up, rainy days were a special treat for my older brother, Rom, and me. We'd clear out all the furniture from the living room and take out a big green box from the closet. We knew that soon our apartment would be filled with ten-year-olds who came over for one reason: to gamble.

When my parents had brought back a miniature roulette and card table from their trip to Italy one year, it was as if my brother and I had found our calling—to run a casino for kids. Sometimes we played for plastic chips, other times for candies or marbles. We always had several games going, but our specialty was cards, from war to blackjack to basic poker.

It was all fun and games until one kid by the name of Yaron showed up. Yaron was upbeat and energetic, but he couldn't stand losing. You'd be in the middle of a game, and if he decided that his chances of winning weren't good, he'd suddenly shout "Tornado!" at the top of his lungs and mess up all the cards. The first time was irritating, the second annoying, and pretty soon you knew that you should never again invite over Yaron and the chaos he brought with him.

Indeed, there's a paradox at the heart of chaos. Left to its own devices, chaos will wreak havoc and destroy everything in its path. However, these great acts of destruction often precede leaps of creativity. The question, then, is whether we can have the best of both worlds. Can we harness the power of chaos without suffering its havoc? Is there a way to use the creative and innovative potential in chaos without unleashing destruction?

The solution, I believe, is something I call "contained chaos." A little bit of chaos, encouraged but confined within borders, can be highly beneficial to an organization's overall health.

Take, for example, Yaron and his card games or, more specifically, poker. A game of five-card draw has a staggering 2,598,960 possible hands. But only 40 of these combinations will yield a straight flush, the highest hand; likewise, there are only 624 possible ways to get four of a kind, the second-highest hand in the game.

Clearly, if we were to bring in Yaron—unbridled chaos—the entire game would be ruined. But what happens to the chances of getting a strong hand if we add *just a little bit* of chaos? I like to think of it as Yaron inside a protective bubble. In this case, what happens to five-card poker if we add to the deck a single joker, a wild card? The effect is extraordinary. You go from 40 ways to obtain a straight flush to 184 possible ways to get the highest possible hand. When we look at four of a kind, the effect of a wild card is even more pronounced: we go from 624 possibilities to 3,120.

Think about that for a second. Adding one wild card, a contained bit of chaos, makes you four times more likely to get a fantastic hand. In the case of the lowest hand in poker, two of a kind, just one wild card presents you with 150,000 more solutions.

Of course, poker, with its statistics, rules, and calculable odds, is one thing. You can't simply add a wild card to an organization. We can't just add Yaron to our team and hope that everyone will behave in positive ways.

We have found, however, that you can isolate *elements* of chaos—white space, unusual suspects, and organized (or planned) serendipity—and that these, in turn, inject a bit of contained chaos to your decision making. Let's take a quick look at each of these three elements.

White Space

If you had visited the Chicago headquarters of 37signals during any given day in June 2012, you'd have seen . . . not very much. The conference rooms were empty, desks sat unoccupied, and the company's lights, in fact, were turned off. You might have wondered if the company had gone belly-up.

A few weeks earlier, CEO Jason Fried had announced that the entire company would "effectively [take] a month off from nonessential scheduled/assigned work to see what we can do with no schedule/assignments whatsoever." It wasn't for cost-cutting purposes or to impose massive layoffs. Taking the month off was actually an experiment in *productivity*.

All employees stayed on salary, but there were no schedules and no assignments, creating an intentional lack of structure; there was just white space. "Our theory," explained Fried, "is that we'll see better results when people have a long stretch of uninterrupted time. A month includes time to think, not just time to squeeze in some personal work around the edges."

It was certainly bold, and the more cynical among us can imagine employees aimlessly surfing the Internet, having long lunches with friends, and catching up on their favorite TV shows.

Indeed, during the first few days, employees just tried to get used to the fact that they didn't have to attend to their daily responsibilities. But soon thereafter, as Fried describes in his column in *Inc.*, individuals from all different parts of the company came up with "a new way to sell one of our products, a better way to keep our customers informed of the status of our systems, a fresh take on surprising customers with better service, and a better way to introduce new employees to the rest of the company. I was blown away by the creativity, polish, and execution."

Of course, not every organization can afford to give its employees a month to do nonessential work. But new findings in neuroscience teach us that we don't need to give people a full month off to engender the creative benefits of white space. Just a little bit can be enough. However, we live in a society that tries to squeeze efficiency out of every moment. In the chapters to follow, we're going to see how Albert Einstein used white space to come up with his most significant discoveries, how schools have learned that recess—unstructured time—improves student learning, and how neuroscientists are discovering that our brains are surprisingly engaged and *effective* when we're in white space.

Unusual Suspects

"We don't 'predict' the election," declared Frank Newport on November 9, 2012, the Friday after the general election in which President Obama handily defeated Mitt Romney. It was one of the last things you'd expect a professional pollster to say. "Nor do we make estimates of the Electoral College." The statement was especially odd considering that Frank Newport was the editor in chief of Gallup. Yes, *that* Gallup.

The Gallup polling group had a healthy dose of egg on its face for wrongly predicting the outcome of the national election. "In the end, Gallup's national popular vote estimate," Newport said in an attempt at justification, "was that the popular vote was too close to call, a statistical tie—50% for Mitt Romney, 49% for Barack Obama. When the dust settled, Romney got 48% of the popular vote and Obama received 50%, meaning that Gallup's percentage-point estimate was within two percentage points for Romney and within one point for Obama." It seemed like the kind of cumbersome excuse you might give for messing up on a project in your college statistics class, not something coming from the nation's most respected polling institution.

What was even more shocking, however, was that Gallup wasn't alone in its errant prediction: it was joined by such venerable firms as Rasmussen Reports,

American Research Group, and Mason-Dixon, all of which wrongly called the election in Romney's favor.

In the months and weeks prior to the election, nearly everywhere you turned you'd see predictions that would prove to be very inaccurate come election day. Failed predictions were seemingly everywhere—except, that is, in the *New York Times*'s blog *FiveThirtyEight*, written by Nate Silver.

Silver not only correctly predicted President Obama's victory in the 2012 election but also projected exactly how many electoral votes President Obama would win and correctly called the outcomes of every Senate race except one, North Dakota.

So where did this statistical guru with the unparalleled political instincts come from? Where did he hone his methodology? Baseball, of all places.

Silver spent six years working with the website Baseball Prospectus, predicting the performance and overall development of baseball players.

Now, while Frank Newport did technically have a point—Gallup *was* in the business of taking the nation's pulse on a variety of issues, rather than actually predicting the outcome of an election—Silver was the one who turned out to be best equipped to do the predicting.

That's because baseball is in the business of foreseeing the future. In baseball—whether you're a manager, a bookie, or a fan—you want to know how a team or a player is *going* to do. You already *know* where things stand *now*—the statistics and win-loss record tell you that. The front office wants to know if it should keep a player or trade him. The manager wants to know if he should bench a player or put him in. Fans want to know if a young prospect is going to help the franchise bring home a World Series title. And gamblers want to know what a team's odds of winning are on any given day.

Nate Silver took what he'd learned in baseball and applied it to politics. At first the idea seemed so out there that Silver actually needed to use a pseudonym, calling himself "Poblano." Why be so coy? Because the last person you'd think of as the go-to person for election predictions is a baseball statistician.

In this book we'll see that Nate Silver is not alone. I call people like Silver *unusual suspects*. Unusual suspects don't seem to belong in the field they're in and tend to weave together seemingly disparate worlds. We're going to look at how unusual suspects have revolutionized a wide array of fields, changing everything from the way we sequence DNA to how we play video games, think about dancing to music, and even work inside a Fortune 500 company.

Organized Serendipity

Lisa Kimball doesn't look particularly subversive. Her hair has retained the reddish hue of her youth, she often dresses in purple, and she frequently wears her glasses on top of her head, occasionally forgetting where she's placed them. When she facilitates small groups, she leans back, one foot out, and observes the participants with a knowing air. You have to look closely to see the subversion; it's the mischief in the corners of her eyes.

Much like Nate Silver delving into politics, Lisa, a former elementary school teacher, seems like the last person you'd recruit to fight a deadly pathogen, one that is responsible for more deaths in the United States than HIV/AIDS.

Methicillin-resistant *Staphylococcus aureus*, or MRSA, is an antibiotic-resistant staph infection, which means that most drugs are ineffective in fighting it. More terrifying still, the easiest way to contract MRSA is to be admitted to a hospital. And as if that weren't bad enough, rates of hospital MRSA infection are rising at an alarming rate.

The good news about MRSA is that it's completely preventable. Hospital staffers simply need to carefully clean their hands every time they see a patient. Seems easy enough. But the bad news, believe it or not, is that getting health professionals to wash their hands is harder than you'd think. It's not that doctors lack personal hygiene; it's that in a busy hospital setting it's hard to *always* stop and clean your hands.

Hospitals first tried to combat the spread of MRSA by educating their staffs. Clearly, the logic went, if people knew that a simple trip to the sink could save lives, you'd have 100 percent compliance. And thus in hospitals across the country up went posters extolling the virtues of the practice. Some were factual: *Stop! Think . . . wash your hands!* Others attempted wit: *Don't let infection get under your skin.* But the message was always the same: *Wash your hands!*

Well-intended though they were, these educational posters—as well as related pamphlets, signs, and buttons—yielded few positive results. "Information doesn't change behavior," quips Lisa. "If it did, none of us would smoke and we'd all floss."

Lisa's philosophy is that instead of trying to enact change from the top down (i.e., print a lot of posters telling people what to do, or attempt to enforce rigid guidelines), we're actually much better off creating little pockets of chaos. The idea is that in this chaos, solutions can emerge. And what Lisa does is try to foster serendipity.

This process of organized or planned serendipity is so subtle that unless you pay close attention, you're in danger of overlooking it altogether.

Lisa will often start by assembling a smorgasbord of people: nurses, aides, administrators, engineers, secretaries, janitors. "It's important to have a diverse collection of people," she explained.

If we were to sit in one of these groups, with different people talking about this or that, we'd be tempted to deem them overly chaotic and unfocused. But that's precisely the point. "It's a little bit like jazz," she says with a smile. "A classical concert is too rigid. Random noise is too unpleasant. You need a few structures, but then you also need to let go."

What's especially interesting about Lisa's methodology is that she doesn't need to tightly manage it for it to be effective. "One of my proudest moments," she laughs, "happened when I *wasn't* there."

After Lisa left one hospital group, the discussion meandered to the proper protocols for bathing people who had been diagnosed with MRSA. "Apparently you should use really hot water," Lisa explained. "But then one of the nurses chimed in and said, 'Well, that's a problem, because on our wing *there is no hot water*.'"

The other members looked at one another in disbelief. This was, after all, a modern hospital. Incredulous, one of the engineers wanted to see for himself. He, along with the nurses and the rest of the group, took the elevator up to the wing in question, stuck a thermometer under the faucet, turned on the hot water, and waited.

Sure enough, the water, which was supposed to be boiling hot, came out ice cold.

Asked how they managed without hot water, the nurses described a process you'd expect to hear about only if you lived in the 1890s. Or in a very poor neighborhood. Or in Romania. "First," said one of the nurses, "we have to go down to the basement with two pitchers to get hot water and bring it back up. But it really takes three full pitchers of hot water to bathe patients, and so we have to make two trips."

Clearly, a lack of hot water was inhibiting infection control, and everyone agreed that something needed to be done. But here was the hitch. At the time, the hospital was undergoing a major renovation, but the wing with no hot water was not due for a renovation for at least another year. A change in the schedule would cost the hospital millions of dollars.

Rather than jump to an immediate solution, however, or—worse yet—twiddle their thumbs as they waited for a miracle, the people in the executive suite opted for contained chaos. They created just a *bit* of white space by holding open meetings and allowing time for reflection. This white space, in turn, fostered an environment where unusual suspects could speak up.

Sure enough, a subsequent meeting happened to be attended by a janitor. He listened with concern as a nurse recounted the story of the nonexistent hot water.

During a pause in the conversation, the janitor cleared his throat and asked, "Are you sure the valve is on?" The nurses looked at one another blankly—no one knew.

Up again to the wing the group went and followed the janitor down the hall to a cluttered closet filled with cleaning supplies. The janitor immediately started clearing out brooms, mops, buckets, even a slop sink, revealing a pipe and valve all the way in the back.

Because the hospital was so old, the paint had chipped off the valve, and the nurses couldn't see whether it was open or closed. Everyone just assumed that if there *was* a valve, it would of course be turned on. The valve squeaked as the janitor turned it. To the group's surprise, they soon heard the familiar sound of water rushing through a pipe—and just like that, the wing advanced to the twenty-first century, with hot water at every tap.

When we take time to reflect, we often see that our organizations have grown so big, so regimented, that we've become mired in procedure, endless meetings, and top-down memos and directives. Meanwhile, the knowledge that could end up saving millions of dollars might very well reside in the least expected of places.

"This wasn't the cast of characters you would usually find on the official task force," Lisa said. "There were no executives in the room. And yet this group uncovered the answer."

How many times, in an effort to minimize chaos, do we inadvertently stifle innovation?

It may have seemed serendipitous that the janitor came to the meeting. And certainly there was a feeling of serendipity that he thought to ask about the hot-water valve, thus solving the problem. But the chances of finding that missing element had been deliberately increased through planning.

Planning serendipity is about engaging as many parts of your organization as possible. It's about listening to people when they tell you that there's a problem and then empowering them to discover the solution. After all, the solution may very well be sitting in the room.

In the chapters ahead, we will look at how loose or open structures allow for greater success, encouraging serendipity in such diverse arenas as business school admissions, online media, and problem solving in all kinds of businesses. These three elements of contained chaos—white space, unusual suspects, and planned serendipity—can help both large businesses and small start-ups to introduce more innovation, drive growth, and propel excellence.

(3)

EINSTEIN'S BRAIN

Letters started pouring in to Switzerland's University of Bern from physicists all over Europe with questions and praise. Some came from the most esteemed scientists of the day. The letters were addressed to one Albert Einstein, who a number of months earlier had published his theory of relativity. But what the letter writers didn't know was that Einstein didn't work at the university. The physicists knew that he lived in Bern and just assumed he was a professor at the university there.

In fact, Einstein had nothing to do with the university. He was a patent clerk. A government worker had turned the world of physics upside down.

We all know the story of how Einstein, at a young

age, made stunning advances in physics. Most of us also have heard that Einstein was a poor student and was able to make his pioneering discoveries in physics despite being completely divorced from academia.

It was almost too extraordinary to believe. A twenty-six-year-old emerges seemingly out of nowhere with a scientific theory that changes the world. That alone would have been unprecedented. But ten years later Einstein once again revolutionized physics, reinventing our understanding of gravity. Today Einstein's name is virtually synonymous with genius.

The explanation that most of us have grown up with for Einstein's breakthroughs is that Einstein had such a brilliant and unusual mind that he—almost magically, in a stroke of insight—saw the universe in a whole new way.

In trying to understand Einstein's unique genius, scientists over the years initially focused on the structural nature of his brain. Einstein had such an extraordinary mind, scientists reasoned, that there must be something fundamentally *different* about his brain.

When Einstein died in 1953, coroner Thomas Harvey removed what had become the most famous brain in history as a matter of course; it was a regular part of the autopsy procedure. What he did next, however—putting the brain in a jar of formaldehyde, slipping the jar into a bag, and walking off with it—was not. But Harvey believed it was his duty to science and to the world to preserve Einstein's brain in order to let researchers study it and unlock the secrets of his mind.

In the succeeding years, neuroscientists, or neuro-anatomists, as they used to be called, asked Harvey for certain sections of the brain in a race to pinpoint exactly which part of Einstein's brain was so unique.

Scientists found that Einstein had a higher-than-average concentration of neurons in the part of the brain responsible for mathematical thinking. This seemed like a promising lead. The problem with this finding, however, was that Einstein wasn't exceptionally gifted in math. His first wife, Mileva Maric, used to check all his calculations and correct them. And while Einstein was far more accomplished in math than your average English—or math—major, his discoveries weren't really mathematical breakthroughs. Instead, his theories of relativity reconceptualized our notions of time and space. They were more a new set of ways of looking at the universe, supported by the math, than a set of complex mathematical formulas.

Another scientist, Marian C. Diamond, discovered that Einstein had more glial cells than average. Glial cells make up the myelin layer that insulates the brain's axons, speeding up communication between the neurons. They also function as a distribution system, bringing energy to the neurons while removing waste.

However, only in one area of Einstein's brain was the difference in glial cells statistically significant. And since Einstein's brain was older than the other brains Diamond compared it against, and glial cells continue to divide as we age, it was only natural that Einstein had more of them. So while his glial network conceivably could have had something to do with his genius, we simply cannot know its impact for certain.

On and on went the physiological investigations. Scientists discovered that Einstein's brain was wider than average. On the other hand, it also weighed less than average.

In the end, the studies on Einstein's brain proved compromised in many ways and yielded no real insight into his genius. The reality is that each of us has unique idiosyncrasies in the makeup of our brain.

Even Einstein didn't think it was his brain that made him who he was. He once commented that the gap between what the public thought of his intellectual prowess and the reality was "grotesque."

But if it wasn't his brain that made the difference, what *did* set Einstein apart? And what does Einstein's genius have to do with chaos?

Einstein the Slacker

At the University of Zurich at the turn of the twentieth century, rows of well-dressed students would have been taking copious notes, smoking, and tackling complex formulas. One student who likely would not have been in the room, however, was Einstein, who was inclined to skip class and hang out in the coffeehouses on the Bahnhofstrasse, talking about new ideas in physics with the café crowd.

In the summer, while other physics students were working in labs or helping professors publish papers, Einstein hiked the beautiful trails of the Appenzell District in the Alps. It was as if his entire year were one big, unstructured interlude.

And that is our first clue to Einstein's genius. To all appearances, Einstein was a slacker. Granted, he was a slacker obsessed with theoretical physics, but he was a slacker nonetheless.

He couldn't be bothered to go to class. He engendered so little confidence in his academic abilities that one of his instructors suggested he give up studying physics altogether. In a great bit of irony, when graduation rolled around, Einstein was the only unemployed member of the class of 1900. His father, Hermann, tried to call in favors to get his son a job, but to no avail.

Imagine his poor mother's desperate concern: "You have to start going to class." "What happened to the intelligent young man I knew?" "You know, if you worked harder, you'd be surprised by how much progress you could make."

It's easy to sympathize with his parents' likely responses. Einstein's seemingly dilettante behavior would have driven most parents to distraction.

But his parents' misgivings were for naught. What Einstein was actually doing was exercising a very special part of his brain.

Most of us tend to have clearly defined ideas about what makes up the road to success. We value discipline and diligence, hard work, and the idea of "paying your dues." Unstructured time just "hanging out" is for teenagers with too much time on their hands, we think, and for surfer bums. Most of us need to pay attention, study hard, and learn.

But that's not what Einstein did at all. As we'll see, Einstein followed a specific *process* in developing his ideas—one intimately related to the chaos imperative. It is one that arguably led to his extraordinary and unpredictable brilliance. And it is one that each of us can tap into as well.

The Tyranny of Structure

Think for a moment of the ideal manager or leader. What attributes would you assign to him or her?

My guess is that you'd say a leader is someone who is able to get things done, someone who is organized and able to give clear guidance to subordinates, someone who is a model of efficiency.

For most of us, a skillful leader or CEO runs a tight ship; the organization is tightly controlled. And no organization is more tightly run, perhaps, than the U.S. Army.

One of the things I came to realize when I first visited a U.S. Army base was that every part of a soldier's day is meticulously planned, with physical training followed by formation, inspections, and meetings.

This same kind of discipline and structure crosses over into many of the soldiers' personal lives. A senior officer I met told me about his routine. "My alarm clock goes off at 0500, I check email, eat a bowl of oatmeal, read the newspaper, and am out the door by 0545. I get to the gym at 0600. I finish the workout at 0700, take a shower, and am at my desk at 0730." He went on to describe the rest of his day, but you get the picture. Just listening to the highly structured nature of his routine can make you feel like a slacker by comparison.

While most of our lives may not be quite as rigidly

organized, the way our institutions, businesses, schools, and other organizations are structured and set up is probably not significantly different. We take training courses and consume books on how to optimize our days; we schedule meetings to maximize performance; we enroll (or are enrolled) in time-management seminars to help us use our time wisely. Corporations are on a never-ending quest to be more efficient and productive, using the latest technological tools. Our children's schedules are equally filled—morning to night, often—with nonstop activities, from school to ballet to football to piano, not to mention traveling soccer team practice and scheduled play dates.

We try to optimize our time and create as much order as possible. The thing is, though, that *we pay a hefty price for optimization*. In fact, we're in danger of snuffing out an essential part of the way our brain functions.

Although well intended, such a heavy emphasis on structuring our lives can stifle creativity, genius, and innovation. And yet, as research by Dr. Marcus Raichle at Washington University and Dr. Jonathan Schooler at the University of California at Santa Barbara's META Lab shows, when we disengage, a special network in our brains turns on and begins to make innovative connections. We will look more closely at this network in the next chapter. For now it is important to realize that our brains need white space in order to think creatively. The same is true for organizations.

Think back to the account of the medieval Church with which we started our story. The Church had become so regimented, so tightly managed, so set in its ways that it precluded creative thought—whether about the natural world or about the human condition. It took a catastrophic event to radically shake things up and overthrow centuries of tradition, which allowed Europe to emerge from its stagnation.

Similarly, if we want to foster creativity and innovation in our own lives, we too need a bit of chaos.

Most of us have been brought up with the idea that the more organized we are, the more effective we'll be (and, by implication, the better we'll be as people).

When I started my work with the U.S. Army, I was amazed by its level of organization. I met with generals who were in charge of massive military programs: the general in charge of the army's boot camp program for new recruits, the general in charge of the Army Reserve, the general in charge of requisitions. They were smart, capable, and fanatically well organized. After all, they were in charge of the expenditure of billions of dollars and responsible for the tens of thousands of men and women under their command.

Inevitably, before every meeting I'd get a frantic call

from a general's aide asking, "What's the agenda for the meeting?"

The first time I was asked the question, I blurted out honestly, "To talk."

"Yes, but what about?"

"How the army is trying to be more adaptive."

"So where are your PowerPoint slides?" the exasperated aide would ask, not having received anything from me in advance.

"I don't have any. The agenda is to talk freely, without a set agenda, and see where the conversation goes."

I came to realize just how structured the world of the army was. And for senior officers in the military, it makes perfect sense. With so many responsibilities, they want to make sure that their time is used efficiently.

But I couldn't help thinking that such a rigid structure handicapped the army when it came to adaptive thinking, being flexible, and encouraging innovation. I needed to convey to them that there is something important in our decision making that happens when we stay *off* task.

Chaos Comes to the Army

After one conversation between General Dempsey and me, we decided to try an experiment to bring a bit of chaos into the institutional army.

I realized how unlikely this all was. General Dempsey, the man in charge of the training of hundreds of thousands of soldiers, who was responsible for tens of billions of dollars, was willing to bring chaos into a system that had been designed since time immemorial to instill order and structure and to keep chaos at bay.

In a very real way, the terrorist attacks of 9/11 had the same effect on the U.S. Army that the plague had on the medieval Church. Twenty years ago, the last thing army generals were doing was sitting around trying to figure out how to bring chaos into their well-oiled machinery.

But in a bold move, General Dempsey recognized that for the system to change, for the army to be able to adapt to the modern battlefield, it needed to introduce what I call "pockets of chaos"—places where structure and efficiency are set aside or blocked off to create a more organic process that allows new ideas to come to the fore.

"You realize," I explained to General Dempsey, "that by definition we won't be able to precisely plan what emerges out of this. We're purposely doing something disruptive. To try to predict what will happen as a result is the antithesis of this. But I do believe that *something* will happen."

General Dempsey understood and agreed. "You know, Ori, I don't have an end state in mind. We don't know what we don't know yet."

In the military world, an end state is the be-all and end-all of a command or order. If you charge a hill, for example, the desired end state is to control the highest ground on the battlefield. If you invade a country, the desired end state is to defeat the enemy and force them to surrender as quickly as possible. No matter what the order is, in order to act, you need an intended end state.

"So we create a program," I told him. "But I need to ask you to send your top guy to this program. If this is going to have a chance of succeeding, we'll need buy-in from the very top."

Without hesitating, Dempsey pointed to an officer in his early forties who was sitting at the head of the table. "Dave, you're going."

Colonel Dave Horan, Dempsey's chief strategist, I would discover, was methodical in his thinking, and when he looked at you, you could almost see the gears of his mind quickly turning over potential scenarios and calculating possibilities.

As Dempsey "voluntold" him to go, I could almost see the calculation in the colonel's eyes. Should he take me down right there?

At that moment, I felt the weight, the responsibility, of what we were about to attempt. Throughout my life, parents, teachers, professors, and bosses had insisted on a clear plan with specific steps to achieve whatever objective I was pursuing. I was about to create and implement an elite, army-wide program that was purposely designed to be unfocused, unplanned, and inefficient.

The End of Recess

A few weeks after my meeting with General Dempsey, I was on a plane to Fort Leavenworth, Kansas, home to one of the army's biggest schools, the Command and General Staff College (CGSC). CGSC is where army officers, usually majors, go to begin learning strategic thinking. It's alumni list reads like a who's who of the U.S. Army: Marshall, Bradley, Eisenhower, MacArthur, Patton, Powell. David Petraeus was its commandant from 2005 to 2007.

I was picked up at the airport by Steve Rotkoff, the colonel who had led the "prayer session" we talked about in Chapter 1, that had predicted the insurgency in Iraq. Rotkoff was now involved with a new army center officially named the University of Foreign Military and Cultural Studies but unofficially called "Red Team University." Learning from what had happened in Iraq, the army was training officers to act when necessary as dissenting voices within their staffs.

The first thing I noticed about Rotkoff was that between his pronounced eyebrows and his swarthy appearance, he would have been the perfect actor to play a mob boss in the movies. It was just a matter of chance, in fact, that he ended up going to West Point instead of accepting an acting scholarship.

Rotkoff had been assigned to develop and execute the controlled chaos program with me. I could tell that although he was very open to new ideas, he had a healthy dose of skepticism concerning what we were about to do. "You know, Ori," he cautioned me in the car, "we're an organization based on structure."

Over the next several years, I learned a great deal about education in the army and its various schools. While well meaning, many instructors in these schools crammed the days full of PowerPoint presentations. At one school, Dempsey issued an order banning the use of PowerPoint in the classroom. The instructors obeyed on the day General Dempsey came to visit, then returned to their slides the day after he left.

As Colonel Rotkoff and I started to plan out what each day of our program would look like, I felt subtle pressure to make things as efficient as possible. We were taking officers away from their homes to an immersive program, spending valuable government money, and working under the watchful eye of the military's top brass. It was tempting to structure the hell out of our days.

It's the same kind of drive, in fact, that we see in our school systems today: the administrative pressure for more efficiency, more structure, and greater accountability.

We can trace the move toward efficiency back to the Supreme Court's 1954 *Brown v. Board of Education* decision, which mandated that the federal government improve educational quality for poor and minority students. But handing down a court decision is one thing. Actually improving quality in schools is another.

In the 1960s, as part of his war on poverty, President Johnson managed to pass the Elementary and Secondary Education Act (ESEA). The meat of the ESEA was in Title I, which gave federal money to states to help them raise the level of education in public schools serving the poor and minorities. In return, the federal government demanded some level of accountability from those schools. To meet these demands, schools needed to create measurable standards. In order for schools to be measured, in turn, school days became more structured; the education process became more efficient.

Although the program was a complete failure, the quest for efficiency continued. In 1983, twenty years after Johnson's legislation was enacted, the National Commission on Excellence in Education released a report under the title *A Nation at Risk* that found that

13 percent of seventeen-year-olds were functionally il-
literate. Among minority seventeen-year-olds, that figure was almost 40 percent.

Worse, the educational malaise was spreading. *A
Nation at Risk* reported declining achievement levels in
verbal ability, math, and science. Only one-third of students could solve a math problem requiring several steps.

The report stood in stark contrast to what was happening overseas. Japanese schoolchildren were held up
as exemplars. They studied diligently, without com-
plaint. They had precocious math skills and strong science and engineering skills, and they outperformed U.S.
students on all the tests. It was clear that the United
States was falling behind.

It was clear that there was something special about
Japan. Indeed, the report recommended turning the
screws even tighter. It called for America to emulate
the Japanese, instituting more rigorous and measurable
standards, implementing a longer school day, and as-
signing students more homework. In order to improve
the performance of American students, we needed even
more structure, more discipline, more time studying and
learning.

Over the next ten years, schools did become more
structured. But things got worse. By 1994, test scores
weren't low merely among poor and minority students;
they had gone down across the board. Schools were

becoming more equal, but in the wrong direction: they were becoming equally *bad*.

Still, the tyranny of structure persisted. Clearly, the thinking went, we still didn't have enough rigor and structure. So President Clinton signed a new education act legislating higher standards for schools and more accountability in the form of test results.

Nonetheless, our schools continued to decline. In 2002, President George W. Bush signed into law his own educational reform with No Child Left Behind. The law basically told the same story and offered the same goal. And it really cracked down on schools this time.

New standards were set for a fundamental core curriculum. Standardized tests would be given yearly to students in order to gauge Adequate Yearly Progress (AYP). The AYP number was how schools would be held accountable. If it was too low, a school could be shut down. In essence, No Child Left Behind was the federal government telling state boards of education, "All right, this time we're really serious."

But an unintended consequence of this system was that school curricula began to narrow. Teachers became fixated on teaching the subjects that were on the standardized tests. At the elementary school level, 58 percent of school districts reported teaching English two and a half hours more each week. Forty-five percent of school districts reported teaching math an hour and a half more each week. This extra focus on math and English was accomplished by eliminating seemingly unnecessary parts of the school curriculum: art, music, and especially recess. If you're trying to improve schools, the thinking went, the last thing you should do is allow kids to have fun on the playground.

Surely all this has led us to finally achieve progress in our schools, right? Yet in 2010, 38 percent of schools failed to make their AYP number, an all-time high. The more the government has enforced efficiency, the more the goal has seemed to recede into the distance. America is currently only thirty-seventh in the world in science education, twenty-fourth in math, and eighth in innovation. Something isn't working.

When we look at countries that are doing well in education, we see some striking differences. The first is a commitment to hiring highly qualified teachers. It's obvious how this helps to create a better learning environment.

But the other difference is much more surprising. In trying to emulate Japan, American schools missed a key point. Along with their rigor, Japanese schools give their students *more* unstructured time. Even with their longer school days and higher test scores, Asian children spend a full 25 percent of their school day in unstructured time.

Could American students be underperforming because they don't get as much free time? Does unstructured time actually increase effectiveness? It is a paradox that brings us back to 1900 and young Einstein.

The Olympia Academy and Discovering Relativity

Einstein barely completed his university studies; graduate school was out of the question. His head was full of ideas, but he had no institutional avenue to pursue them. His mind was engaged with the great physics questions of the day, but he was locked outside the gate of the academic citadel with its labs and lectures.

His situation was similar to that of another young man who took time off during his freshman year: Thomas Jefferson. For most people, Jefferson brings to mind images of powdered wigs, fiery declarations, a restless curiosity, and a zealous interest in things scientific, intellectual, and political. But if you'd met Jefferson as a young man, you'd have encountered a different person altogether.

Jefferson neglected his university studies during his freshman year and hung out with horse traders, card sharks, and actors. During his sophomore year, however, he was taken in and mentored by George Wythe, a lawyer. Wythe was good friends with the governor of Virginia, Francis Fauquier. Wythe brought young Jefferson with him to the governor's house.

Dinner at the governor's house (sometimes referred to as the "palace dinner") was an entertaining affair, an intellectual free-for-all where guests celebrated learning, discourse, and the exchange of ideas.

It was there—in this loose, chaotic, unstructured environment—that Jefferson learned about the Enlightenment thinkers and began to formulate his own political philosophy. He once said that the dinner table at the governor's house was his true university.

Albert Einstein, however, had no one to bring him to dinner at the governor's house.

When he submitted his dissertation, he was asked to withdraw it because it criticized professors' theories. So he was left on his own to ponder the great scientific questions of the day. In essence, Einstein found himself with an inordinate amount of white space—unstructured time that had nothing directly to do with the formal task of studying physics. Yet this white space may have proved instrumental in the formulation of Einstein's theory of relativity.

Einstein created his own rag-tag team to serve as a kind of informal graduate school, which he called the

Olympia Academy. The group was made up of Einstein, Michele Besso, Conrad Habicht, Maurice Solovine, and Einstein's wife, Mileva Maric.

All were incredibly smart, of course, but they were also slackers in their own right: perpetually late, forgetful, and disorganized.

On a typical day, they would meet at night and eat a simple dinner of bologna, cheese, yogurt, and fruit. They would plan on reading from and discussing a book, but they rarely got more than one page in before they started arguing.

The members of the Academy didn't merely argue over the latest advances in physics and other scientific discoveries. Just as often they read philosophy and the arts. It was a course of study Einstein would not have been able to pursue within the confines of a university graduate program in physics. In contrast to graduate students at universities, Einstein had no undergraduate students to teach, no papers to grade. He had no senior faculty directing his studies or university politics to deal with.

The intellectual white space the group enjoyed was reflected in their use of actual physical space. The Olympia Academy roamed. On warm nights they'd walk the old stone arcades of Bern and make their way to the river. Other evenings they'd climb to the top of Mount Gurten, lie on their backs contemplating the heavens, and talk until dawn. In the morning they'd make their way back down and sit at a café fueling themselves with coffee and ideas. Some workdays they'd all meet again for lunch at Café Bollwerk, where they could continue arguing and discussing.

Let's take a moment and think about how Einstein's life would have looked had he entered graduate school. Imagine him working in that relatively rigid environment, trying to make a name for himself and be taken seriously. Not only would Einstein's days have been filled with grading papers and attending faculty meetings, but his ideas about relativity and gravity would have been disparaged. They were so outside the norm, so crazy, that his fellow physicists would have stopped him in his tracks and tried to redirect him into "serious" work.

Instead, Einstein was surrounded by fellow dreamers. And it was this band of seemingly directionless outsiders who would help him to come up with the theory of relativity.

Educational Pockets of Chaos

In 2009, researchers at the Albert Einstein College of Medicine published their analysis of the daily routines of eleven thousand third-graders in the United States. They found that three in ten children either had no recess at all or enjoyed only a minimal break (less than fifteen minutes) during the day. Think about how little white space these kids were given.

African American and Hispanic children were even more likely to be deprived of recess, as were children who came from lower-income families or who had less educated parents.

The reasoning behind this trend is best summarized by Benjamin Canada, former superintendent of the Atlanta school district, who argues that it is common sense that reducing recess time positively affects achievement.

Imagine two classes of third-graders across the hall from each other. Both are preparing for upcoming standardized tests in math and reading. One teacher follows common sense, extending the school day and limiting recess to a couple of fifteen-minute sessions per day. The students in this class stay at their desks and study hard. They're drilled with worksheets and exercises. Day after day they push with intense focus through the material in the curriculum.

The teacher across the hall takes a more counterintuitive approach. This teacher also extends the school day, but it is broken up. Every forty minutes the children are given ten minutes of free time—of white space. During this time they are allowed to hang out, run around, talk to their friends—to do whatever they feel like. They are allowed to self-organize. They play games. They get into disagreements and try to work them out. They make friends.

Which class do you think would do better on the tests?

Common sense tells us that the class that worked harder would do better. When most of us think of economically disadvantaged schools, we think of unruly kids, wasted time, a lack of discipline, paper airplanes and spitballs flying about. If these kids are to succeed in the future, we think, we need to give them as much structure and discipline and precious education as possible.

But common sense, in this instance, is wrong. What the research tells us is that the second class, the one with more white space, will come out on top.

In the Albert Einstein College of Medicine study, the researchers discovered that the children with more recess time learned more, developed better emotional and cognitive skills, were healthier, behaved better, and managed stress better.

The study's principal investigator, Romina M. Barros, MD, said, "We need to understand that kids need a break. Our brains can concentrate and pay attention for 45 to 60 minutes, and in kids it's even less."

Yet it's unnerving for teachers to provide white space for the kids, because they feel they're not doing their jobs. It's equally tempting for politicians to banish white space in the name of efficiency and economy. Can you imagine a politician running on a platform of "more un-structured time for students"?

But the seeming aimlessness that comes with such white space—Einstein hanging out with his friends in a café or Thomas Jefferson engaged in meandering conversation over the dinner table—is actually crucial for our brains. In fact, there is no empirical evidence to support Benjamin Canada's statement that reducing recess time raises academic achievement. What the data *do* tell us is that if we want our children to learn more and perform better, the school day must have class time woven together with free, unstructured time—white space.

For one thing, breaks lead to better behavior and better learning. Anthony Pellegrini and Catherine Bohn, in their paper "The Role of Recess in Children's Cognitive Performance and School Adjustment," found that children, especially boys, were far more attentive in class after a period of recess and that children were less attentive when there were long stretches of time between recess periods. Breaks every fifty minutes led to better behavior and better learning.

Moreover, such white space needs to be protected from the organized structure of the rest of the day. In another study, Pellegrini noted that the kinds of social interactions children have with one another during recess, often without a grown-up involved, are more complex and socially challenging than the interactions they have under the direction of a teacher. The skills children develop in this social white space, in turn, help them develop their cognitive skills. Pellegrini discovered that the social behavior of kindergartners was an excellent predictor of their academic performance in first grade. Learning to maneuver in the social world on their own at recess helps children develop complex thinking, as well as learn to handle stress better.

Back in the 1980s and 1990s, when Japanese students were far outpacing American students on standardized tests, Harold Stevenson, professor of psychology at the University of Michigan, decided to study Asian elementary schools to find out what they were doing differently. One of the most important elements he found, as described in his book *The Learning Gap*, written with James Stigler, was that "the long school days in Asia are broken up by extensive amounts of recess. The recess in turn fosters a positive attitude towards academics."

Asian students actually enjoyed school more and suffered from fewer of the ailments often associated with stress. As Pellegrini did after him, Stevenson found that with more recess, Asian students paid more attention to the teacher. While the Asian school day is indeed longer, almost all the additional length is made up of free time.

Rather than try to replicate Asian teaching methods, American schools might do well instead to study their recess practices.

These recess studies have dramatic implications for all of us, even if our school days are long behind us. The *New England Journal of Medicine* recently conducted a study on leisure activities and the risk of dementia in senior citizens. Physical activities such as bicycling, swimming, or playing golf, while very good for the cardiovascular system, didn't help at all in reducing the risk of dementia. But there was one notable exception that left researchers scratching their heads: dancing.

According to the study, dancing lowered the risk of dementia by a staggering 76 percent. What is it about dancing that's so different from other physical activities? One might conjecture that it is the music that makes a difference. But you can jog with headphones, listening to your favorite music, and still not gain the benefits that people get from dance.

Could it be the sociability of dancing? While sociability certainly was a plus for seniors, Richard Powers, a Stanford professor who is an expert on social dance, realized that the researchers had not examined what *kind* of dancing the senior citizens engaged in.

The dementia study began in 1980 with subjects ages seventy-five to eighty-five. As Powers describes it, "Those who danced in that particular population were former Roaring Twenties dancers (back in 1980) and then former Swing Era dancers (today), so the kind of dancing most of them continued to do in retirement was what they began when they were young: freestyle social dancing. I've been watching senior citizens dance all of my life, from my parents (who met at a Tommy Dorsey dance), to retirement communities, to the Roseland Ballroom in New York. I almost never see memorized sequences or patterns on the dance floor."

In essence, the seniors were engaged in the same type of creative activity as the Asian schoolchildren. The kind of dancing they did wasn't rote, memorized, highly structured dancing but the freestyle, improvisational, white-space-style dancing of the 1920s, '30s, and '40s. Professor Powers concludes that the constant decision making that freestyle partner dancing forces upon us— making little decisions and predicting the movements of a partner—builds neural pathways. Doing the same steps over and over again doesn't help our brains remain vibrant, elastic, and vital. It doesn't challenge our thinking. Doing the same thing day after day doesn't help us sustain or build new neural pathways. Participating in activities that force us to improvise and think does.

In the same way, young children on the playground find themselves challenged by social-cognitive demands that don't occur in the classroom. Children are more likely to disagree with one another in the relative social chaos of recess than they are to disagree with a teacher in the structured classroom environment. When they disagree, they are confronted with someone else's point of view. They are forced to try to understand their friend's perspective and deal with the consequences.

Just as children need to learn math and reading, they need to learn how to function in social settings, when they're *off* task. At recess, children learn skills such as deciding which game to play, choosing a game leader, resolving conflict, and finding ways to interact with others. An amazing amount of social enculturation happens in such unstructured settings. How children do at recess, in fact, is a good predictor of how they'll do in school.

It's important to note that researchers aren't proposing school days without an agenda, a lesson plan, or rules. They are not suggesting daylong chaos (which sometimes can be a struggle to avoid in an elementary school). Rather, they are suggesting discrete units of unstructured time—discrete pockets of chaos—throughout the day to help students learn better.

In 1903 most of Einstein's Olympia Academy cohort moved away. But Einstein's good friend Michele Besso took a job at the same patent office. The Olympia Academy had shrunk to conversations between Einstein and Besso as they walked to and from work together talking about physics. But it was a time that gave Einstein the freedom and space to think differently.

Here is how journalist Dennis Overbye, in his book *Einstein in Love*, describes Einstein's experience: "From the standpoint of the established physics community Albert was an outsider, a dabbler who worked at the patent office and browsed the journals on the side. From his own standpoint Albert had no expectations and nothing to lose. He had no mentors and no favors to pay back. Seemingly he had no fear. He could afford to be radical."

In other words, Einstein could conceive of something as radical as relativity *only in* the white space of his life outside academia. All those years of being on his own outside the structure of a university program, with lots of time and the constant exchange of philosophical and scientific ideas, enabled Einstein to make the great leap in thought that gave us modern physics. It allowed Einstein to see the world in an entirely new way.

So what did Einstein actually see?

It all had to do with the question of how light moves through space. Specifically, if there is no air in space, how can light move through it?

Scientists at the turn of the twentieth century

believed the answer was something called "ether." A concept borrowed from Aristotle, ether was believed to be an odorless, colorless, tasteless, and weightless essence that pervaded the universe. Ether was what light was believed to move through.

The only problem with the ether idea was that, try as they might, scientists could not actually find ether.

That summer when Einstein was hiking the Alps rather than doing an internship for a professor, he first allowed himself to consider the notion that perhaps there was no ether. Perhaps electromagnetic waves—light—moved through empty space.

In 1901 a young scientist named Max Planck, in a desperate effort to get his math to work, suggested that perhaps light moved not in waves (like sound) but rather in discrete packets called quanta. Einstein agreed. Assuming that light was made up of tiny particles like grains of sand, Einstein began to imagine the way energy might move.

Wandering the streets of Bern with his friend Besso and going over the math with Mileva in their garret, Einstein pondered how to explain the universe if light moved through empty space at a constant speed. And was it possible, he asked himself, that the universe had no center, no foundation?

Everyone from Aristotle to Newton had assumed a central, immutable stage on which the universe acted out its play. But, unable to find that central stage—the ether—Einstein asked, what if our reality only exists *relative* to the motion of other things? What if there is no still point, no horizon? What if the only way to explain the dynamics of energy is to say things only exist relative to one another?

It was in white space that Einstein, a self-described heretic, an outsider, found the room to pull the rug out from under the universe's feet. It all came together for him one spring day when he went to see Besso.

All day they discussed the ins and outs of the problem of light moving through empty space. Einstein was so frustrated at the end of the conversation that he left, telling Besso he was giving up the search entirely. He went home to bed, and then, in the white space between waking and sleep, the solution suddenly came to him. He returned the next day and told his friend, "Thank you. I've completely solved the problem." Einstein spent the next six weeks laying out the math and the argument for his special theory of relativity, which posited that we do not live on a central, shared stage, that our reality is relative to everyone else's.

Einstein published his paper in the physics journal *Annalen der Physik*, thinking it was too bizarre to submit in pursuit of his doctorate.

Two years later, still working at the patent office,

Einstein was leaning back in his chair when "all of a sudden a thought occurred to me. If a person falls freely he will not feel his own weight. I was startled." That was the beginning of the general theory of relativity, in which he theorized for the first time that gravity could bend light, that gravity could actually twist space/time, and that black holes might exist.

Notice that there's a pattern to Einstein's process of discovery. He first imagined a world without ether while hiking through the Alps. His special theory of relativity came together while he was falling asleep. And his general theory of relativity came to him while he was leaning back in his chair at the patent office. In none of these instances was Einstein focusing on physics per se.

Computer Science or Calligraphy

One theory about why white space is so important in our thinking is that our brains engage in two kinds of attention: direct (as when we're in class) and indirect. Allowing the brain to flow from one state to the other is what creates optimal performance.

World-famous painter and inventor Leonardo da Vinci constantly switched pursuits; he was an astronomer, a painter, a scientist, and a military strategist. One can argue that it was by weaving together these different disciplines that he was able to come up with such novel inventions.

Apple founder Steve Jobs pursued many different interests on his path to creating and later reestablishing the Apple brand. For example, in college he developed an interest in calligraphy, a subject that would seem to have little to do with computer science and design. Yet here is how he described his experience learning calligraphy in a talk he gave to the graduating class of Stanford University in 2005:

> Reed College at that time offered perhaps the best calligraphy instruction in the country. Throughout the campus every poster, every label on every drawer, was beautifully hand calligraphed. Because I had dropped out and didn't have to take the normal classes, I decided to take a calligraphy class to learn how to do this. I learned about serif and sans serif typefaces, about varying the amount of space between different letter combinations, about what makes great typography great. It was beautiful, historical, artistically subtle in a way that science can't capture, and I found it fascinating.
>
> None of this had even a hope of any practical application in my life. But ten years later,

when we were designing the first Macintosh computer, it all came back to me. And we designed it all into the Mac. It was the first computer with beautiful typography. If I had never dropped in on that single course in college, the Mac would have never had multiple typefaces or proportionally spaced fonts. And since Windows just copied the Mac, it's likely that no personal computer would have them. If I had never dropped out, I would have never dropped in on this calligraphy class, and personal computers might not have the wonderful typography that they do. Of course it was impossible to connect the dots looking forward when I was in college. But it was very, very clear looking backwards ten years later.

Think about Jobs as a young student seeking the advice of a career counselor. Would any counselor suggest that instead of taking courses on computer science, he should explore calligraphy? Yet that unstructured foray into an unrelated field paid a wealth of dividends a decade later.

Similarly, had Thomas Jefferson sought the help of a career coach about the best path toward becoming a political activist and the leader of a new country, few would have suggested long dinners chatting about philosophy.

And who would have recommended that Einstein hang out with other physicists discussing philosophy?

Of course, the outcomes of including such pockets of chaos in our lives are far from predictable. Almost by definition, they can't be. Nonetheless, as I was about to discover in working with the army and with Steve Rotkoff and Dave Horan, factoring in white space when working on a project can lead to some eureka moments.

Circles in the Army

A couple of months after I visited Steve Rotkoff in Kansas, it was Steve's turn to come to the Bay Area, my neck of the woods. "You know, Ori," Steve said as we walked along Telegraph Avenue in Berkeley toward the University of California campus, "I've been to many places in the world I'd never thought I'd visit. But I never, *ever* expected to be having lunch at the UC Berkeley faculty club." We were there to meet with Cort Worthington, a good friend of mine who is one of the most popular professors at UC Berkeley's Haas School of Business, where he teaches leadership courses.

Over a lunch of tofu salad, I told Steve and Cort, "The reason I wanted to get you together is that I think we need to teach the army officers about white space."

Normally, as plans are discussed, Rotkoff breaks out a green hardcover notebook, in which he keeps meticulous notes of every meeting and conversation. Tucked away in boxes at his house are all the notebooks he's ever written in since the 1970s.

After lunch, we headed back to Cort's office to talk. As Cort stood at the whiteboard, Steve opened his notebook to a fresh page.

"So what we're thinking about," Cort began, "is a weeklong module."

"Sounds good," Steve said. "What's the schedule?"

Using a thick blue marker, Cort wrote up a calendar on the board, with a column for each day of the week. "I'm thinking we'll have three sessions a day," he said as he continued to write. "One session from nine to twelve, then lunch from twelve to one. Right, Ori?"

I nodded. An hour for lunch seemed about right.

"We can then schedule a session from one to four, and from seven to ten p.m.," Cort continued as Steve meticulously copied every word into his notebook. "In the first session, we'll organize ourselves into a circle."

Cort drew a circle inside the allotted time period. Steve followed suit.

"In the second session, we'll have another circle." Steve made another circle notation in his notebook.

"Hold on," Rotkoff said. "What do you mean by a *circle*?"

Cort and I looked at each other, and Cort said, "Well, we'll sit in a circle."

"What do we talk about?" Steve asked.

"Whatever the group wants to talk about."

"Do you lead off the discussion?" Steve asked, trying desperately to make *some* sort of sense out of this.

"Oh, no," Cort said, almost offended. "No. Our job is to let the group find its way." And with that he continued laying out the schedule. "In the third session, we'll have another circle." This pattern continued for Tuesday and Wednesday, as Cort drew a circle in each session.

Rotkoff looked at the board filled with circles with an expression that suggested he was looking for the hidden camera. "You mean you want to spend an entire week sitting in a circle?"

"Not the entire week," Cort replied. "We'll also have lunch and dinner."

Later that afternoon, as we drove back to San Francisco, Steve tried to be diplomatic with me. "This is a government program, and I'm in charge of making sure that the government is spending its resources appropriately. Remember, we're going to have combat veterans in our group—they've served in Iraq and Afghanistan. They're busy people."

"And you want to make sure that we're not going to be wasting their time," I interjected.

"I have a notebook with the schedule, and all it has in it are circles!" he exclaimed in frustration.

I knew that the circles would be much more substantial, not an exercise in futility. Tempting as it was to structure the group's time, I was convinced that the white space inherent in the circles we were planning was going to yield some very dramatic outcomes.

It all comes down to the fact that when we regiment our days too severely, when we stay completely focused on one task, our minds tend to stagnate after a time. I had become convinced that we need white space in order to avoid becoming so task focused that we lose our creativity.

To better understand these moments—to understand why white space is so essential—let's take a step back and look inside the human brain. To the surprise of neuroscientists, there appears to be a whole area of the brain that flourishes when we let a bit of chaos into our lives. It's what allows us to solve problems in a novel way.

(4)

THE NEUROBIOLOGY OF INSIGHT

From Twisted Buildings to the Periodic Table

It was to be architect Frank Gehry's first skyscraper—a New York City building that would rise seventy-six stories into the air. Located at 8 Spruce Street in Manhattan, it would be the tallest residential building not just in New York but in the Western Hemisphere. However, Gehry was stuck.

Known for his highly distinctive designs, from the Guggenheim Museum in Bilbao, Spain, to the Walt Disney Concert Hall in Los Angeles and the Experience Music Project in Seattle, Gehry creates buildings that look like they popped out of the imagination of a man obsessed with Dr. Seuss's books or *Alice in Wonderland*. Wrapped in unexpected materials such as titanium, they billow and bulge in ways buildings are not supposed to. Gehry's signature is to give his buildings movement; they appear to have been caught in midflow, as if they were on their way somewhere else. The Gehry-designed Hotel Marques de Riscal in Elciego, Spain, is famous for a curving, swooping titanium roof that looks like a giant has just awakened and is stretching, with the bedcovers falling down in massive folds. When first encountering a Gehry creation, people often become giddy, awed that such a thing exists. The apartment building he designed in Prague, known as "Fred and Ginger," has two rounded bays that rise leaning into each other, like dancers.

Gehry's buildings are one-of-a-kind works of architecture. Their budgets are typically high, and each is intended to be a showpiece in its own right.

But the skyscraper in New York presented a unique set of obstacles: a limited budget, very little space, and, most important, the challenge of creating a Gehry showpiece out of that most mundane of architectural pursuits, the condominium.

While Gehry could easily indulge his whimsy in creating a museum, the same wasn't true for the condos at 8 Spruce Street.

When architects think of a modern apartment building, they typically don't think great art. Apartment buildings put function above form. Their purpose is to house as many people as possible as efficiently as possible.

Gehry's proposed new condo was no exception. The apartments—ranging from studios to three-bedrooms— were designed to be rental units. The developer had to squeeze as many dollars as possible out of every square foot of space, especially in the wake of the Great Recession.

Gehry employed many architectural tricks, such as making the tower relatively tall and thin, giving the visual impression of a more sophisticated and less bulky building. But none of these gave the structure Gehry's signature attribute: movement.

The architect's first idea was to give the Spruce Street tower a twist, like that of a nine-story building he had designed in Hanover, Germany. That building looks as if a giant grabbed it from the top and turned it clockwise. The structure, though made of steel, bends and twists as it rises.

But it's one thing to twist a building; it's another to twist plumbing for seventy-six floors of apartments stacked atop one another. Simply put, it was too difficult to put in plumbing that could accommodate a twisted tower. Mundane water and sewage pipes stood between Gehry and his grand vision.

How could he make the building fantastical but still incorporate the plumbing lines the building needed?

Gehry couldn't crack the problem, despite playing repeatedly with the design. He tried making the building rounder, more flowing, but nothing worked.

In a way, Gehry was in a predicament similar to that faced by nineteenth-century Russian scientist Dmitry Mendeleev. Mendeleev was a professor of chemistry at the University of St. Petersburg who was also involved in a host of pursuits in the fields of geology, physics, and economics.

Sitting at his desk in 1869, Mendeleev was agonizing over a chemistry problem. At the time, the field was still in its infancy, with only sixty-three known elements.

For years chemists had been trying to create some sort of order, make some sort of sense of the elements. Why was it that elements such as iron rusted if wet, while gold and aluminum seemed impervious to damp conditions?

Mendeleev set himself the task of finding the underlying rhyme and reason. He meticulously studied the known elements and their properties, immersing himself so deeply that he stayed up for nights at a time trying to find a pattern, but without success. Like Gehry, Mendeleev was tackling a massive problem, working relentlessly to solve it.

Put yourself in their shoes for a moment. You've been working hard on a project for a long period of time, yet you've encountered a problem that you just can't crack.

You are convinced there's a workable solution, but you are stuck trying to find your way to it. You feel a mounting sense of frustration, but you can't solve the problem, nor can you let it go.

What would you do? Would you try to block out all distractions, so that you could take on the problem mano a mano? Would you make a list of all the challenges you face and try to deal with them systematically, one by one? Would you talk to friends, colleagues, and experts to see if they had any fresh perspectives or ideas?

Most people's natural inclination, of course, is to work harder, to concentrate even more intensely, to tackle the issue head-on.

But imagine, for a moment, surrendering to the chaos inside you. In that very moment of surrender, could a eureka moment find you? It turns out that our brains are actually *wired* to provide these kinds of sudden insights and eureka moments. New developments in neuroscience give us a surprising look at the mechanism behind this.

The Noise That Wasn't Noise

For years scientists have been trying to figure out what parts of the brain handle different kinds of tasks, from reading to recognizing friends. The introduction of the fMRI—a magnetic resonance imaging scan of a working brain—in the 1990s gave researchers a peek at how our minds operate.

For example, subjects undergoing an fMRI were shown pictures of their spouse, as scientists tried to pinpoint the specific part of the brain responsible for sexual attraction or love. Or they would be shown a scary movie, so researchers could see what part of the brain becomes active when we are afraid.

But scientists became so preoccupied with what we do when we're intently focused on a task that they ignored the whole picture. Their working hypothesis of the brain was that it was basically like a car. As in a machine, different parts play different roles: Broca's area controls speech, the amygdala is linked to the fear response, the neocortex is in charge of conscious thought, and so on.

When you turn off a car, you expect its various components to shut off as well. Likewise, scientists thought that when people are not focused on a specific task, those parts of their brains turn off as well, or at least quiet down in terms of neural activity.

But it turns out that isn't necessarily the case.

Scientists discovered that when a subject inside an fMRI machine was off task, the part of his or her brain that had performed the task would go quiet—the electrical impulses that the fMRI reads as neural activity

would diminish. But then they found something unusual. While the part of the brain focused on the conscious task went quiet, another part of the brain would
suddenly spring to life. Why was the brain "lighting up"
when it wasn't doing anything? This occurred as subjects
stared blankly at crosshairs while they were doing nothing, so researchers referred to this sudden spike in electrical activity as "noise," assuming it was as meaningless
as the white static on an old picture-tube TV. Initially,
researchers developed sophisticated computer models to
tune it out.

But what if this wasn't mere noise? What if it wasn't
random electrical outbursts getting picked up by the
machine? Was it possible it was something else entirely,
something essential to how our brains work?

Neuroscientist Marcus Raichle at Washington University in St. Louis became curious about "noise" in the
brain.

So he and other neuroscientists started examining
this neural activity. And they uncovered several important clues that would prove critical to understanding the
neuroscience behind white space.

Dr. Raichle noticed the first clue when he looked at
studies meant to discover what happened in the brain
when people concentrated on a task. To establish a
baseline, subjects were placed in an fMRI machine and
told to simply "keep their eyes closed, to relax, to refrain

from moving, and to avoid any structured mental activity such as counting, rehearsing, etc." The scientists took careful note of the brain activity in this state. Next, subjects were asked to focus on a specific task involving concentrating on an image.

Dr. Raichle looked at the difference in brain energy generated by subjects when they were off task versus when they were focused on a specific task—that is, the difference between when the machinery of the brain is on (i.e., when we're concentrating) and when it's supposedly turned off. For example, imagine you are sitting in a chair reading in the afternoon sun. You lay the book on your lap and start to think about something you read, but soon your mind is wandering; you're daydreaming. Then you come back to the task at hand, pick up your book, and begin to read again. The question is, how much more energy does your brain use when you start to read again than it did when you were daydreaming?

The surprise, Raichle found, is that there was virtually *no* difference in the amount of brain activity between the two states—when subjects were intently focusing and when they were just letting their minds wander. The difference between the amount of energy your brain uses while daydreaming and the amount it uses while focusing intently is less than 5 percent.

How much of the brain's overall potential is used when you daydream? Anywhere from 80 to 95 percent.

In other words, when you're daydreaming your brain is operating at nearly full capacity!

When the subjects were again given a specific task, the diffuse brain activity quieted down. So clearly *something* was going on during that time when the brain was not focused on a specific task. And clearly the brain was spending a lot of energy on this process, whatever it was.

Dr. Raichle noticed a second clue too. Time and again, exactly the same places in the brain lit up whenever a subject was not engaged in a specific task—when the person was in "white space." Ten regions of the brain, including the posterior cingulate cortex (responsible for episodic memory), the precuneus (also responsible for memory, as well as for reflection and consciousness), and the ventral anterior cingulate cortex (responsible for emotions) lit up with activity.

The *same* regions of the brain were active each time; moreover, the regions seemed to be communicating with one another. Was it possible that the background neurological chatter wasn't noise at all?

But there was a third clue as well. When Raichle studied the fMRI images, he discovered that the central hub of these regions of the brain had two separate blood supplies, making it far less vulnerable than most parts of the brain to damage from a stroke or concussion.

The human body tends to reserve redundant blood supplies for those organs that perform critical tasks, such as the liver or kidneys. "It's an insurance policy," Raichle said. In Raichle's view, it signified that this region of the brain was critically important.

Dr. Raichle began to realize that what he was looking at was actually a vital brain process. It appeared that the regions of the brain that were lighting up actually constituted a network bridging various parts of the brain. This was where brain activity defaulted to when subjects weren't concentrating on a specific task, when their brains were in white space. Raichle named it the *default mode network*.

But it was the fourth clue about the default mode network that really shook up scientists' understanding of the brain.

The Problem-Solving Machine

We tend to think of the human brain as the most organized machine that evolutionary biology has ever produced. It has a host of specially honed regions involving language, memory, and logical thought that are activated when we're given a task. Approaching the human mind this way, scientists assumed that when we lack a task, part of our brain is idle.

But our brain is similar to our other organs, including the heart and kidneys. When we go to sleep they keep working. And it turns out that the brain spends a lot more time in default mode than we'd ever imagined.

When neuroscientists studied the default mode network over extended periods of time, they noticed that it didn't shut off. As long as the subject was in a relaxed, daydreaming state, the default mode network was active.

This part of the brain kicks in when we're staring into space. Or when we let our minds wander as we walk or drive. Or when we are going to sleep. Or as we wake up.

In fact, the network is always on *unless* we are focused on a task. That is, the default mode network is always engaged, unless we actually *interrupt* it to perform a specific task. We're constantly engaged in a process that is ungoverned by conscious thought.

So why does the brain devote so much effort to something so seemingly random, chaotic, and unproductive?

To answer this question, look around to your left and right, wherever you are right now—at a coffee shop, on a plane, on a subway or train. As you read these words, your eyes are taking in an extraordinary amount of information. Approximately 10 billion bits of visual information, in fact, hit our retinas every second. Of those, only 6 million bits actually make it through to the optic nerve. Of those 6 million, a mere 100,000 bits make it all the way to your visual cortex.

And of these, *just 100 bits* actually connect to your conscious mind. Think about how tiny that ratio is.

Our conscious minds are only aware of 0.000001 percent of the information that hits our eyes.

Of the billions of synapses in the visual cortex, less than 10 percent are actually dedicated to processing the stream of visual information that our eyes take in. So what are the other 90 percent of the synapses doing? And how do we make sense of the world around us when so little of the visual data our eyes take in makes it into our conscious processing?

The answer is that most of what we know and understand about the world comes from internal processing. We use our memories, our ability to infer the whole from the parts, our narrative sense of ourselves from the past to the present, and our ability to imagine the future to fill in the gaps in the external data we process. We use that other 90 percent of our synapses to *understand* the world.

That is, our brain has an internal story of what the outside world looks like. Visual information merely conforms to or contradicts the story. Meanwhile, the narrative is constantly changing and evolving as we take in more information.

This ratio—between the amount of energy we expend taking in visual information and the amount of energy we spend processing it—is key. What scientists are discovering is that our default mode network is continually constructing an internal narrative. It asks questions about what we've taken in: *What does this mean? How does it differ from past experiences? Which experiences is it like? What does it mean will happen in the future?*

For example, let's say that you're presented with two very compelling job offers. One is a creative position in an up-and-coming company where you'd work under a supervisor. The other is for a less interesting company, but you'd have more authority to make your own decisions. You make a list of the pros and cons of each and talk to your friends about which one you should take. Which one better fits your personality and your future goals? You're still undecided when, during a walk, it comes to you: a memory of being back in high school or college, taking great satisfaction in finishing a project you initiated. Your default mode network has kicked in, linking your new job offers to experiences from long ago in your past. It's the default mode network that gives us a sense of our life story and makes connections between those experiences that we can't easily make when we're focused intently on a specific task.

Our brains construct these narratives, the ones that we use to guide our decision making, while we are in white space—while we're daydreaming or in relaxed mode. Dr. Yvette Sheline of Washington University describes it this way: The default mode network is where we "contemplate the future. It is where we survey our own internal milieu, what is going on inside us. It is where we plan and anticipate."

In other words, the tremendous activity in our default mode network is our brain weaving together the immense amount of data that we take in every day. It not only decides what's important to keep and what's not but also bridges and ties together different narratives, making sense of the world.

The thing is, though, that the network functions spontaneously. We can't control or predict what connections it will make. And that's the beauty and the benefit of white space. In white space, our brains create new connections and novel solutions that wouldn't come to mind if we were intently focused on a task.

Take the French novelist Marcel Proust, sitting in his mother's house, with nothing to do but enjoy a small ladyfinger-like pastry known as a madeleine placed in front of him. He takes a bite, and suddenly his default mode network is off and running, turning sensory inputs into episodic memories—that is, creating narrative out of his life.

The taste reminds Proust of an episode years ago when he bit into a madeleine as a little boy. More memories are retrieved. They're placed into a narrative flow of his past moving toward his present. He sees meaning in his life. The memory and the meaning bring up a tremendous amount of emotion, because the default mode network is connected to the way we process emotions. In an unconscious process, the madeleine has triggered a torrent of conscious memory, meaning, and narrative, all seemingly in a flash. But it is a flash only to Proust's *conscious* self.

His default mode network has been connecting these memories, ideas, and feelings for quite some time.

What was essential to sparking the chain of connections was the moment of being off task. It was the white space of having nothing to do but eat a madeleine that created the opportunity for all this information to flood into Proust's mind. This doesn't mean that if we daydream all day or sit around idle all the time, somehow a magical part of the brain will be activated, leading to breakthroughs or moments of genius. Rather, it means that after long periods of hard work, we sometimes need to relax and let our minds wander to allow the unconscious default part of our brain to synthesize and consolidate all we've been working on, to help us discover the meaning and the way forward.

The Default Mode and White Space

To understand the power of the default mode network, we have to look at the parts of the brain that connect to form the network. The posterior cingulate cortex (PCC) is a part of the default mode network's central hub. The PCC plays an important role in retrieving memories, especially autobiographical memories. But the PCC does something else even more useful.

As neuroscientists describe it, the PCC is constantly evaluating how the environment around us is changing, and based on that information, it helps us make new decisions. The PCC is constantly analyzing the data we've taken in and asking, *Has the world changed enough to warrant a new approach?* If the answer is yes, then the PCC motivates us to change our behavior. It is what signals us to adapt.

The PCC alerts us that markets are shifting, that our employees need a new challenge, that our spouse is unhappy. It is an unconscious mechanism built into our brains that's far more efficient than conscious thought. But without white space, the PCC can't tell us what it knows. We need to be off task, in white space, in order for this part of our brain to work.

Another hub of the default mode network is the precuneus (PC), which gives us the ability to reflect on ourselves and compare our traits to those of people around us. So one part of the default mode network, the PCC, allows us to compare episodic memories with current data, and another part, the PC, allows us to reflect. To see how the two work together, let's go back to Frank

Gehry's dilemma with the condominium he was designing on Spruce Street in New York City.

Gehry was staying up late wrestling with the problem
of making a condominium look like a Gehry building.
Then, one night, he had a massive realization. "I had
one of those eureka moments," he said, "at three o'clock
in the morning, when I thought of Bernini."

We are in love with the idea that innovation comes
to creative people in a flash. The ancient Greeks had the
notion of a muse visiting us with inspiration. Creativity
seems to hit us like a bolt of lightning.

It's tempting to think that such eureka moments are
a flash of genius, random ideas that somehow enter an
individual's mind. But given what we know about the
default mode network, we now have a more compelling
explanation. Ideas actually bounce around in our heads
for a long time before we become aware of them.

Gehry had first seen the statue of St. Teresa by the
Baroque master sculptor Bernini decades earlier, at the
age of thirty.

St. Teresa was widely recognized for her spiritual vi-
sions, the most dramatic of which involved a fiery angel
who plunged a flaming spear into her heart, leaving her
in exquisite spiritual pain and consumed by a great love
of God. Bernini, famous for capturing the most dramatic
moment in a myth or story and with an uncanny ability
to make marble come to life, depicted the saint in this

moment of ecstasy, her eyes half closed, her mouth open, and even her robes animated by the force of her feeling.

Bernini's sculpture sits in a small chapel in a Roman church, Santa Maria della Vittoria. You can see the sculpture only during mass, and even then you have to make your way to the very front pew, lean forward, and turn your head just so to peek into the little chapel where it sits. Gehry recalled, "I don't know how to do the crossing myself very well. The young priest was howling with laughter when he saw me in the front row, trying to kneel when everyone else kneels, but doing it wrong."

The architect did manage to see the sculpture, and what stayed with him for decades afterward were the elegant, flowing folds of St. Teresa's robe. And that was the image that came to him decades later at three o'clock in the morning.

In the middle of the night, as his mind wandered, Frank Gehry's default mode network made a connection. More to the point, his default mode network retrieved the memory of Bernini's statue and saw the association to be made with the current problem. Then it recognized that this was the adaptation necessary for the building at 8 Spruce Street.

Using the image of the Bernini folds, the architect realized how he could solve the condominium problem. He would make the building a regular straight-walled condominium, with Bernini-like folds laid over the building's exterior to create his signature flowing style.

Instead of twisting the entire building, Gehry created bay windows, each stacked slightly to the right or the left of the one below it, giving the impression of a waterfall cascading down a cliff. The finished building stands 867 feet high yet looks like it is made of liquid.

Gehry had the pieces of the puzzle inside his brain the whole time. But it took the white space of 3:00 a.m. insomnia for him to let go of his conscious focus on the problem. Only then could his default mode network kick in, reaching back into his memory, retrieving the image of the Bernini folds, and associating them with the problem of 8 Spruce. And it happened to Gehry all at once. Our conscious minds experience this unconscious process as "Eureka!"

The Aha

In the mid-1960s Gary Starkweather was a researcher at the Xerox Corporation working on high-speed fax machines.

Xerox was a copier company—its products took images that already existed and copied them. "One day in 1967, I was sitting in my lab looking at all of these big mainframes," Starkweather said, "when I started thinking, 'What if, instead of copying someone else's original, which is what a facsimile does, we used a computer to generate the original?'"

Or as Starkweather recalled later, "One morning I woke up and I thought, 'Why don't we just print something out directly?'" In an effort to get enough light on the paper so that the machine could create the image, Starkweather turned to the new technology of lasers. As a result of his work, he went on to invent the laser printer.

The story is reminiscent of Einstein's account of his discovery of his general theory of relativity. He was at work in the patent office, leaning back in his chair, when he realized that if a person falls freely, he will not feel his own weight. With that, Einstein was on his way to redefining how people thought about gravity and space.

Starkweather's account of how he first thought of laser printing is not so dissimilar to what happened to Dmitry Mendeleev.

After staying awake for three nights in a row working on the underlying order of the elements, Mendeleev couldn't keep his eyes open. Reluctantly he put his head down and started to drift off.

As he did so, his default mode network kicked in. And suddenly Mendeleev was able to see the elements arranged in perfect order. When he awoke, he started writing furiously.

His insight was to arrange the elements according to their atomic weights. All at once, everything clicked into place. It was the number of protons and neutrons, he realized, that determined an element's properties— why gold will never rust or why lead is so dense.

As Mendeleev created his table of the elements, he intentionally left open spaces. Those were the places, he figured, where chemistry would discover *new* elements.

Mendeleev published what we know today as the periodic table of the elements in 1870, to a great deal of skepticism. Five years later, however, the element gallium was discovered, sitting right there in one of Mendeleev's empty spaces. Mendeleev's table was not just a description of existing elements; it was a road map to new elements.

Einstein experienced a similar eureka moment in May 1905 when he looked at his friend Michele Besso, threw his hands up, declared defeat when it came to solving the riddle of time and energy, and went home to sleep. When he woke up the next morning, everything had fallen into place, and he began to write his special theory of relativity.

Now, clearly neither Mendeleev nor Starkweather nor Einstein could have arrived at his solution had he not spent considerable time thinking about the particular problem and mastering his field. But in order to solve the problems they were working on, they needed to create a bit of white space. As Mendeleev drifted off, his default mode network sprang to life, gathering up all the information he'd absorbed, connecting it with previous facts and stories, engaging in problem solving and future thinking, and synthesizing all he knew into an elegant solution. The default mode network kicks into gear when we are about to sleep or wake up, when we are at play or daydreaming. And it may be responsible for one of the most profitable ideas the world has ever seen.

Back when Google was still a start-up, its founders knew that advertising was a clear road to profits. At the time, click-through advertising (that is, advertisers paying Google every time a user clicked on an ad) was being touted as the way forward. What seemed so lucrative was that advertisers were willing to pay more per click in order to get their ads more exposure at the top of the list.

But there was a significant problem with this revenue model: Google made most of its money only when consumers actually clicked on the ads. What if an advertiser paid a lot per click to gain good placement but had an unappealing ad or undesirable product? No one would click the ad, and consumers wouldn't even see the potentially more appealing ads that had lower placement. So Google instead decided to give pride of place to the ads that were more likely to get clicked on. If an advertiser paid less per click but was ten times more likely to get its ad clicked on, its ad was given more exposure. This small shift—that the ads had to be relevant—took AdWords from a million-dollar idea to a multibillion-dollar idea.

How did Google come up with this idea? According to one account—which may or may not be apocryphal—two engineers were in the Google offices shooting pool when it came to them. You can imagine the scene: one of the engineers leaning over the table, cue in hand, focused on his shot, the other engineer standing by idly, staring off into space, not focused on anything, his default mode network churning through the problem he'd been working on for months. Dr. Yvette Sheline of Washington University would say the engineer's default mode network was problem solving, anticipating, and contemplating the future while surveying all the engineer's thoughts and feelings. Suddenly a solution appeared—the advertisements had to be relevant.

We are all familiar with the experience of having a sudden insight, of having our unconscious mind crack a riddle we've been working on for some time. That is why, whether urban myth or truth, this story keeps being retold: because it is so familiar. Some people tackle a mindless task such as doing the dishes when they have a problem to solve; others take long walks or a shower or watch mindless television. It is only now that neuroscience has found the mechanism behind this all-too-familiar phenomenon.

J. K. Rowling has described staring out the window of a train that had gotten stuck on the tracks between Manchester and London. Her pen had run out of ink and she was too shy to borrow one. As she stared out the window, an idea came to her.

"I really don't know where the idea came from," she said later. "It came. Just came . . . fully formed. I was on the train when I suddenly had this basic idea of a boy who didn't know who he was. He was a young boy attending a school of wizardry. It started with Harry, then all these characters and situations came flooding into my head."

And so Harry Potter was born.

Such stories give the impression that innovation happens all of a sudden, with little work involved. But that is not true. J. K. Rowling had been writing stories since she was six years old. Mendeleev had been working on a chemistry textbook for three years. Einstein had been stewing over the problems of the universe for more than a decade. Gary Starkweather's life had been focused on optics. Frank Gehry had been wrestling with 8 Spruce Street for an agonizingly long time. And for all of them, the default mode network had been synthesizing the information they were taking in.

But they got wind of it only when they entered white space.

Of course, the default mode network presents managers and leaders with an apparent catch-22. As a manager, when you put your people on a task, are you shutting off their innovative brains? We can't just wait for the default mode network to present eureka moments. As we have seen, it operates best after we have worked hard, gathered facts, and considered approaches. But when a solution doesn't present itself, we shouldn't just buckle down and work harder. What the neuroscience suggests is that at this point we need to step back. We need to give ourselves a little white space.

The Afternoon Walk

When I was nine years old, my family moved from a suburb of Tel Aviv, Israel, to El Paso, Texas. My father was going back to school as an electrical engineer.

For my older brother and me, moving to Texas was an adventure. But for my parents it was a huge gamble. They left behind their families and friends and everything they knew; withdrawing their savings from the bank, they rented a small apartment at the edge of the Texan desert.

Each day my dad would wake up at six in the morning,

study, join us for a quick breakfast, take a bus to school, come home and study again, eat a quick dinner, and study till ten or eleven at night.

It's hard to imagine how my parents were able to balance raising a family with all of his coursework.

But there was another, equally important part of my father's routine. Each evening, as the sun finally set and the hundred-degree daytime temperatures dropped down to more reasonable levels, he'd go for a hike.

I'd often join him on these hikes, walking the narrow paths in the hills and mountains near our house. We didn't talk much, and the scenery—cactuses and an occasional jackrabbit—wasn't much to look at.

My dad didn't make any breakthrough discoveries on those walks. He didn't invent a new way to organize the elements or come up with the plot for a bestselling fiction series. But I'm sure that the white space he enjoyed and the activity of his default mode network played a role in enabling him to keep up with the work.

Not long ago my dad retired from a long career in electrical engineering. On a recent visit I asked him about those walks. He took a long moment to reflect on them. Then he simply said, in the way only an engineer can sum things up, "Those walks were just essential."

Those precious minutes of white space—whether they result from long walks or recess for elementary school students—are critical to our mental health because they give our brains the opportunity to process the vast amount of information we take in. But too often today, our inclination when we need to solve a problem is to think that we must further immerse ourselves in brainstorming and studying, working harder and longer and more efficiently.

If you had to finish a major project for your company next week, how would you plan your time? Would you work through lunch and into the evening? Assign your team members tasks to split up the work? Focus intensely without distractions?

My guess is that the last thing you'd think about—the thing that would seem almost embarrassing to consider—would be to give yourself time to daydream and disengage, to insert a little chaos into the planning process, to consciously carve out some unstructured white space where you could just let your mind wander for a time or go for an aimless walk.

Remember, neuroscientists originally thought of our brains as if they were cars, where regions of the brain, like engines, turned on when they were needed and shut down when not in use.

That model is from the industrial age, when it was common to think of employees working on an assembly line as interchangeable parts of a larger machine. Managers were managing bodies in an effort to make their numbers. Over the course of an eight-hour shift a certain number of products needed to go out the door. Quality and efficiency might suffer somewhat over time, but the assembly line would continue to function.

But in the information age, the paradigm for managers has shifted from managing bodies to managing minds. It is true that a body at rest is a body that is not producing. But a mind at rest could be a manager's, and a company's, greatest asset. Employees who are working ceaselessly on a problem may not be giving their brains the space they need to synthesize information and come up with insightful solutions.

Think of the elementary school students from the previous chapter and the importance of unstructured recess. The same managerial philosophy of efficiency prevails in our businesses. Whether at work or in school, individuals *need* that unstructured time for their minds to perform optimally, to synthesize the vast amount of information they are inundated with.

Creating White Space in the Army

In considering a new program, the army has an unofficial standard known, informally, as the "front page of the *New York Times* test." That is, what would happen if information about the program leaked and made it to the front page of a national newspaper? How embarrassing would it look? And, more important, would anyone be reprimanded or forced to resign as a result?

When we looked for a location to house our experiment, the city of Augusta, Georgia, came out on top, largely because it passed the *New York Times* test with flying colors. Apart from the crowds in early April for the Masters golf tournament, Augusta isn't exactly known as a tourist destination. Moreover, a program located there certainly doesn't sound like a boondoggle.

Steve Rotkoff went to Augusta to scout potential hotels to house the participants and host the program. To meet government standards, he needed at least three bids, so he visited a number of prospective locations.

Rotkoff carried with him a complex spreadsheet listing the different attributes of each hotel: location, comfort of the rooms, quality of the gym, and so on. He gave a different weight to each category depending on how important he thought it would be to an officer: a gym was very important, comfort of rooms less so.

When I landed at the Augusta airport, Rotkoff was beaming. "I found the ideal hotel! It suits our needs perfectly. It's centrally located, it's clean, and the gym is to die for."

"Great," I said. While there are many things I enjoy in life, exploring hotels for a conference isn't one of them. To my mind, the more quickly we decided on a hotel, the more time we'd have to explore the town.

The next morning we stepped into the expansive lobby of Augusta's outpost of a highly regarded hotel chain. Everything in the hotel was clean and modern. The rooms were large, the staff friendly and eager to help. The gym was well enough equipped to be suitable for a professional athlete. And the facility where we'd meet was akin to any large meeting room in any respectable chain hotel. It's where you'd expect to find a conference for an important organization's managers or leaders.

"Next," Rotkoff said, "we're going to visit the Partridge Inn. I wanted to do a quick drop-by, but the lady invited us to take a full tour and I thought it would be rude to turn her down." Rotkoff went on to say that the Partridge Inn was on the wrong side of town, it was far away from everything, and its gym consisted of a couple of exercise machines from the Nixon era.

As we drove out toward the Partridge Inn, the view from our car windows quickly changed from a clean, modern downtown to streets and storefronts that were more run-down. The inn used to be a big draw in Augusta, but it had fallen on hard times. The carpet was worn, the stairs creaky, and the ceilings uneven where the building had started to settle. We went from room to room, nearly getting lost in the labyrinthine hallways. And yet there was a charm to the inn. It seemed like a place where you could lose yourself, rather than just get lost.

Over lunch at the Partridge Inn's restaurant, I turned with trepidation to Colonel Rotkoff and told him, "You're going to hate me."

"Why?" he asked.

"I think the Partridge Inn is better for our purposes."

"Are you serious?" he asked me in surprise, clearly wondering if I was pulling his leg.

"I mean, *feel* this place," I said, trying to explain.

"I don't know what you're talking about," Rotkoff said abruptly as he pulled out his decision matrix. The matrix clearly showed that the other hotel was superior in every way.

"What about these comfortable nooks you can hang out in?" I said, attempting to sound convincing. I pointed out that the officers could sit by the outside pool (with, granted, its peeling paint) or look out at the city view from the large balcony.

We went back and forth: the decision matrix versus what Steve Rotkoff labeled "vibe." Of course, the army at its core is a decision matrix kind of organization—it takes a given action because it makes logical sense, not because of someone's gut feeling. And yet, whether it was my nagging or my vow to take the hit if the Partridge Inn turned out to be a failure, Rotkoff relented.

Two months later, Rotkoff and I were setting up for the first day of class. We had twelve participants coming from various army bases. In the back of my mind was

the worry that they would show up, look around the eccentric locale, shake their heads, and ask, "How exactly
does this help us win wars?"

After trying to arrange the room this way and that,
Rotkoff and I finally agreed on a horseshoe formation,
where all the members could see one another. We set up
long tables, each with a pitcher of water and plenty of
room for participants to spread out their notes and reading materials. Then I went to bed, planning to wake up
early the next morning and get in a workout on one of
the rickety treadmills.

One of the great things about the army is that no one
is *ever* late for a meeting. Ten minutes before we were
scheduled to begin, all the participants were in their
seats, pens in hand, ready to begin the day.

After some quick introductions, it was time to get
started.

"I hate to be a turd in the punch bowl," said Dave
Horan, the guy whom General Dempsey had sent to attend the program. Sitting with his hands crossed and
chewing Skoal tobacco, he didn't look happy. "I thought
the idea for this experiment was to do something different. And here we are sitting around tables. Whatever
happened to your goddamned circles, Ori?"

In an effort to not attempt anything that seemed too
over the top, I had forgotten that the whole purpose of
the experiment was to introduce chaos.

"You're right," I said. "Grab a table and move it to the back of the room. Let's sit in a circle." Another nice thing about working with army personnel is that they do what they're told.

Rotkoff seemed oddly comfortable. It was the first of many times that I appreciated how flexible and open to new ideas he could be, given that he had spent more than thirty years in an organization that was so focused on structure and formality.

Over the next several days, the dynamics and tenor of the group began to shift. Having the time to engage in casual conversation and to walk around the inn or to sit quietly outside made all the participants more reflective.

When Cort Worthington arrived from UC Berkeley several days later, he received a warm if guarded welcome. He began the day with some fun improvisational exercises. The point of the exercises wasn't to make sense but rather to leave behind the vestiges of structure. After an hour or so of these activities, we asked the participants to spend twenty minutes reflecting on two simple questions: *How do you typically act in a group?* and *What, if anything, do you want to work on?*

We didn't expect the questions to have a great deal of impact, but that's where the magic started. One member talked about how he had been relentlessly teased as a teenager. Another talked about a bomb exploding right in front of him in Afghanistan. Yet another described what it was like to be attacked while driving in a long truck convoy.

Some stories were harrowing, others hopeful. But they were all emotionally vivid, rich, and honest. One day, a rather quiet participant spoke up. "You know, something interesting happened last night. It was the first time in four years that I slept a full night. I've had these nightmares, and until last night, I couldn't sleep."

He told us a story about his third tour in Iraq, when he and a small team were ordered to clear a building. When his best friend, standing in front of him, opened the building's door, he was shot and killed instantly.

"I've never been able to shake that memory," he told us, "that image of him lying in front of me. I think something about this group . . . something is helping me start to come to terms with it all."

Everyone was silent. After several minutes, Dave Horan spoke up. "You know, we've been an army in constant war, and the pace has been unbelievable. I mean, don't get me wrong, I'm committed to serving. We all are. But we just haven't had time to reflect."

The army, by being so focused on efficiency, had virtually eliminated white space in the lives of its officers. Imagine what it was like for them to endure such violent and often deadly experiences without having the opportunity to digest what had happened. But in Augusta, with just a bit of time to embrace the concept of unstructured chaos, unusual ideas and bottled-up emotions emerged.

The participants encountered one aha moment, for example, over the terrible problem of suicide in the army. It was the third year in a row in which the military had lost more soldiers to suicide than to combat. Instead of putting returning soldiers who had finished their tours of duty in large auditoriums, where they're given a lecture and told not to attempt suicide, why not put them in small support circles like the one we were having in Augusta?

Another idea that was suggested had to do with the long, barely comprehensible manuals soldiers receive about how to conduct every single aspect of combat. Do you want to cross a river? There's a page in the manual for that. Want to enter a new town? There's a page for that. Need to change a tire on a truck? Yep, there's something in the manual for that as well. What if, somebody said, the army started its own version of YouTube, where instead of manuals, soldiers could demonstrate visually how to conduct simple tasks? Rather than having to read pages explaining how to change a tire on a truck, soldiers could watch a minute-long video showing them how to perform the task. How much easier would that be for the average eighteen-year-old soldier?

Each of these ideas came up after a period of white space, of casual downtime. Yes, the officers in our program had years of training, combat, and leadership experience. But the white space they got at the Partridge Inn, the ability to engage their default mode network, was integral to digesting that experience and relying on it to conjure up new, creative ideas.

The bottom line is that our brains have an amazing ability to solve problems—once we're not focused on a specific task. But we need to let this natural process unfold. We need to *interrupt* our logical problem solving and engage our default mode network. It's often in those moments when we cede control, when we put down that pen, when we fall asleep, or when we talk offline, that true eureka moments seem to find us.

(5)

SURFING NAKED

From LSD to PCR

Joe Neilands, the renowned UC Berkeley biochemistry professor, looked me in the eye and said, "We're going to have a problem."

I squirmed in my chair. Joe was greatly respected in his field, and I feared I had offended him with my request. He had first arrived at the university in 1951 and soon became an institution championing social causes, from traveling to North Vietnam during the Vietnam War to document human rights abuses to (successfully) taking on the university and the largest public utility in California. When I'd first shaken his hand, I had noticed that one of his fingers was missing—an injury he'd sustained while building his house with his own hands.

I had come to Neilands as an undergraduate to see if he'd be willing to be my academic advisor. To say I was nervous was an understatement. The endless rows of graduate students hunkered down over their test tubes and microscopes in the lab were intimidating; potentially breakthrough science was being conducted before my eyes. By the time I found myself sitting in his office, I had broken into a sweat at the thought of making my request. What if he turned me down?

"The problem is," he went on, "I don't give a rat's ass about the bureaucracy of this university. As far as I'm concerned, you can take whatever classes you please. So I don't know how much I can actually *advise* you."

My relief that he wasn't angry at me or turning me down was so great that I let out a short laugh. "That kind of advice," I replied, "would suit me perfectly."

Over the succeeding years, Neilands became a mentor and a friend. Whenever I came to his office, he'd share stories about his most recent political crusade or the latest discovery in biochemistry. But one thing that Neilands said has stayed with me for years.

Early on I made an offhand comment about protestors in Sproul Plaza and how out of control the situation seemed. "I wish they weren't so eager to protest," I told

Neilands. "It seems like Berkeley has been overrun by the counterculture."

Seeing the look on his face, I instantly knew that my words had upset him.

"To me these protests are a field of a thousand flowers," he said. "I say, let them all bloom." He put on his coat and hat, stood up, and continued, "Let me show you something."

I followed him down the corridor to a lab filled with beakers, tubes, and metal tables. "Of all the dozens of graduate students who've come through this lab, only one has received the Nobel Prize: Kary Mullis."

Kary Mullis, he told me, grew up in Lenoir, North Carolina, and went to college at the Georgia Institute of Technology, where he majored in chemistry. In 1966 he was accepted into the biochemistry PhD program at Berkeley.

"Back in the day, he'd sit there in the corner of the lab and concoct chemicals that got him into all sorts of trouble. He tried to synthesize LSD; he even nearly blew up the entire building one day. The faculty was up in arms. They gave me a ton of trouble over him. I just told them to mind their own goddamn business."

Mullis publicly claimed to have been visited by alien life-forms. He liked to surf . . . naked. And he was one of the few scientists to openly question whether AIDS was caused by the HIV virus.

Cal Berkeley was one of the most prestigious science research institutions in the world, and Mullis seemed to be thumbing his nose at it. He might very well have been kicked out of school. Instead, Joe Neilands took him under his wing and offered him the white space he needed to conduct his work.

When Mullis graduated, scientists were making huge strides in studying DNA. The problem they faced, though, was that it's very difficult to study a single strand of DNA. They needed to collect large samples. This, of course, limited the usefulness of DNA in situations where only a small sample was available—say, a tiny drop of blood at a crime scene.

One day, while driving along California's Pacific Coast Highway, Mullis had an aha white-space moment, one that would earn him the Nobel Prize in chemistry. It led him to come up with a way to easily replicate a single DNA strand into thousands or even billions of identical copies. The procedure is called *polymerase chain reaction*, or *PCR*.

PCR is the genetic equivalent of selecting and copying a line of text in a word-processing program. The first step is heating the DNA to near boiling. This causes the famous double helix to unravel and become two separate strips of genetic code.

Next, geneticists select the part of the DNA they want to copy and highlight it. Instead of using a mouse and clicking the cursor over a line of text, geneticists use oligonucleotides (or oligos)—laboratory-synthesized short segments of DNA that match the start and end points of the bit of DNA to be copied. As the temperature of the liquid is lowered, the chosen oligos bind to the section of DNA the scientist wants to copy, as if they are highlighting it.

As the temperature is raised again, an enzyme called Taq polymerase binds to the oligos. Essentially it is like hitting "control-C" on your keyboard to copy a piece of text. The Taq polymerase then adds nucleotides to create a new long copy of the DNA segment—it's like hitting "control-V" and pasting the copied text. The scientists now have a full copy of the DNA segment they chose. Repeat this process thirty times and you have more than a billion copies of the DNA segment.

If you've ever seen an episode of *CSI* where detectives find the murderer by locating a tiny hair, or if you've ever read about geneticists finding a mutation responsible for a disease, or if you've ever known someone who's been screened for a genetic disease, then you've come face-to-face with the results of Mullis's discovery.

Here is how Mullis explained the process of discovering PCR. "In Berkeley it was a time of social upheaval and Joe Neilands was the perfect mentor to see his people through it with grace. We laughed a lot over tea at four every afternoon around a teakwood table that Joe had brought from home and oiled once a month." It was an environment very different from the rest of the labs on campus. Neilands gave Mullis the same kind of academic freedom he later gave me in choosing courses.

"As long as I wrote a thesis and got a degree," Mullis recalled, "he didn't care what else I did, and I stayed in his lab happily, following my own curiosity even if it carried me into music courses, for as long as Joe thought we could get away with it."

Think about how absurd this must have looked to other faculty members: two eccentric scientists having tea in their lab while discussing music and philosophy. Many of us would have been shaking our heads. What Mullis comes to show us, however, is the importance of white space, particularly when paired with people I call unusual suspects or renegades. Unusual suspects are often people who would normally be excluded from an organization for being too different or for holding views considered too extreme or out of the mainstream.

In medieval Europe, the white space created by the plague allowed humanists, who were outsiders or unusual suspects, to be integrated into the system. Their ideas may seem relatively ordinary today, but at the time they were sacrilegious. Normally the Church clergy of the time would not have had anything to do with them, just as the other professors in UC Berkeley's biochemistry department wanted nothing to do with Kary Mullis and just as Einstein's physics professors wanted nothing to do with him. Chaos allows such people to be given a chance. And having adequate white space to pursue their ideas gives them room to flourish.

The point here isn't merely to celebrate diversity. Yes, diversity of thought is helpful to an organization. But what we're talking about here is often something more extreme: people who would make many of us truly uncomfortable.

Joe Neilands passed away in 2008. Before he died, Joe and I reflected back on that day in Berkeley when we saw the protest on the plaza. "All through my career," he said, "my colleagues viewed me as this odd guy with all these outlandish causes, giving refuge to all these crazy grad students in my lab. Now they take pride in Mullis. But at the time they wouldn't touch him."

Unusual suspects such as Kary Mullis aren't necessarily easy to tolerate. They are often outsiders and iconoclasts, and occasionally they can seem downright crazy. But at times it is to our benefit to bring into the fold people who seem to have no business in an organization.

The Guerrilla and the Video Game

Hearing the story of Kary Mullis, my mother interrupted me in her Israeli accent. "So, you're telling people they should hire crazy people into their company? They're going to start shooting people, and then you'll get blamed."

I found myself defending Mullis. "He's not *crazy*, he's just unusual . . . for the situation he was in."

"Making drugs in a laboratory isn't normal," my mother retorted, and that was that.

I'm sure that, had she met him, my mother would have much more likely approved of a man by the name of Shigeru Miyamoto. Growing up in Japan, Miyamoto wanted to be a painter or a puppeteer; he'd always been a dreamer and an artist.

Miyamoto's college career was similar to Einstein's— undistinguished. He attended a school for industrial arts and crafts but went to class only half the time. He spent most of his time looking for a banjo player, as he had fallen in love with bluegrass music and wanted someone to accompany him on his guitar. It took him five years to graduate.

Also like Einstein, when Miyamoto finally graduated, his dad stepped in to lend a helping hand. The father contacted an old friend who happened to be the CEO of Japanese video game maker Nintendo.

It's important to remember what the video game industry was like when Hiroshi Yamauchi, Nintendo's CEO, did his friend a favor and took a meeting with his son. Picture what a typical arcade game looked like in the late 1970s: a single screen where two moveable bars bounced a moving "ball" back and forth or where a player attempted to direct a similar-looking bouncing ball to break through a series of blockades. By the early 1980s the industry had graduated to crude, pixelated characters.

These video arcade games were becoming all the rage. Kids the world over were lining up, quarters in hand, to play Space Invaders and Pac-Man. Those quarters, millions of times over, translated into huge profits, and a mini video game boom was under way, with companies vying to make the next big arcade hit.

Nintendo was not yet in that market. But it had already found success with a home entertainment system named "Color TV Game," and the company figured it could use its technology to come up with a successful arcade game as well.

Within the industry, Nintendo was viewed as an engineering powerhouse. After all, creating video games was basically an engineering feat that involved bringing together hardware (the game console and its parts) and software (the game itself).

Yamauchi had little interest in hiring someone with a degree in industrial design, such as Miyamoto. Yamauchi quipped, "I need engineers, not painters." Nonetheless, he agreed to meet Miyamoto as a favor to his old friend, and in the end he offered him a job as a staff artist. The company had never had a staff artist before . . . nor did there seem to be much need of one in a digital world of moving rectangles and bouncing balls.

Put yourself in Yamauchi's shoes. How should Nintendo try to compete in the arcade game market? Well, of course, by creating a better console.

And that's exactly what Nintendo did. Yamauchi formed three teams—competing with one another—to optimize the console. They focused on engineering solutions, things such as better screen resolution and improved graphics. Miyamoto, meanwhile, was relegated to an apprenticeship in the planning department, where he designed a couple of the drawings to decorate the sides of arcade game consoles. The closest Miyamoto got to game design was to create the illustrations for a game Nintendo was developing called Radar Scope.

If you've never heard of Radar Scope, don't worry—you're not alone. It was a variation on a theme popular at the time, in which the player had to shoot down monsters or aliens that, for some inexplicable reason, were hell-bent on destruction. There was nothing special about Radar Scope, and the game was largely a failure.

But just as the tumultuous times at UC Berkeley in the 1960s offered an opportunity for Kary Mullis to work in Professor Neilands's lab, Radar Scope created an opening for Miyamoto.

Thus, a short time later, in Redmond, Washington,

two thousand Radar Scope consoles sat unplugged, cast aside in the midst of a flurry of video game innovation. Trying to recover from the failed effort, Yamauchi called Miyamoto into his office and informed him that he needed a new game. The head engineer of one of the research teams, Gunpei Yokoi, would oversee Miyamoto, but otherwise he was given free rein. His instructions were simple: convert Radar Scope into a game that kids would want to play.

The aspiring artist had been let loose in the engineer's world. What happened next has become the stuff of legend.

Removed from the fierce competition between the three R&D groups at Nintendo, Miyamoto began with his own ideas about game design. He believed that video games should be treated like stories. He envisioned what no one up to that point had thought about—making games that would cause the player to experience *emotions*.

For Miyamoto, video games were an opportunity to take the characters from his flipbooks and comic books and bring them to life.

It's a simple idea. But it was an idea that no one in the video game world had thought of before.

The first thing he did was to speak with Yokoi and learn what the technological constraints were, given the technology of the day.

In the course of his conversations with the engineers,

Miyamoto began to conceive of a new type of hero, a figure with red overalls, a red cap, and white gloves to make him stand out on the screen. He had stocky arms to better highlight his movement. Miyamoto gave him a hat and a bushy mustache, because animating hair and mouths was still very difficult. All of these were attempts to work within the constraints of the video game world and simplify the game.

Miyamoto also came up with a story for the game. The hero climbed up a half-finished building in an attempt to save his girlfriend, who had been kidnapped by his pet gorilla. Whimsical as it sounds, there was a back story: the hero had mistreated his gorilla; to get back at him, the pet had stolen his master's girlfriend.

Miyamoto thus gave the world Donkey Kong.

When Nintendo's American sales reps were first shown the new game, they were horrified. Steeped in a culture of shoot-'em-ups, they simply couldn't imagine how this game could succeed. One rep actually started looking for a new job. But Donkey Kong, of course, would prove to be Nintendo's first blockbuster hit.

Following this success, Miyamoto was entrusted with his own creative team and given a very clear mandate: create the most imaginative video games anyone had ever seen.

He started with his overalls-clad character from Donkey Kong. This time he imagined him trying to save a princess. But rather than climbing a building, Miyamoto had him running through a landscape.

Miyamoto's innovations were of two distinct types.

First, in this new game the screen wouldn't be still. Rather than a static maze the characters maneuvered through, the screen would roll and players would enter new scenes, new territories, and new worlds. The second innovation Miyamoto imposed was that this new game, like Donkey Kong, was story based.

Miyamoto described his creative process this way:

> What if you walk along and everything that you see is more than what you see—the person in the T-shirt and slacks is a warrior, the space that appears empty is a secret door to an alternate world? What if, on a crowded street, you look up and see something appear that should not, given what we know, be there? You either shake your head and dismiss it or you accept that there is much more to the world than we think. Perhaps it really is a doorway to another place. If you choose to go inside you might find many unexpected things.

While it seems like a no-brainer today, the innovation of weaving an emotionally based story into the game was revolutionary at the time. As Will Wright, the creator of the highly popular Sims games, has said of Miyamoto, "He approaches things from the player's point of view, which is part of his magic." The engineers simply looked at what they could do cheaply and within their technological constraints. Miyamoto, as an unusual suspect in the video game world, asked, *What do the players want us to do?*

What Miyamoto grasped long before other game designers and software engineers was that games should have *emotional* resonance. And his new game, Mario Brothers, was even more successful than Donkey Kong.

Miyamoto followed that with The Legend of Zelda, another blockbuster. The titular character was named for F. Scott Fitzgerald's wife, Zelda Fitzgerald. Not many other engineers and designers in the gaming world were drawing from literature. To date, The Legend of Zelda has had sixteen sequels.

An outsider—a renegade, an unusual suspect—completely revolutionized the video game world. Miyamoto's influence can be seen in the most successful games of today, from Call of Duty: Modern Warfare to Grand Theft Auto and the Sims series. Each creates whole worlds for players to explore, characters for them to identify with, an unfolding narrative to the game. The games have become far more sophisticated, but their general structure still builds on Miyamoto's insight.

Weaving Together Two Worlds

Miyamoto performed two roles within Nintendo. The first was, like Kary Mullis, to bring a new, previously unheard voice into the fold. The second was to weave together two different worlds that had previously been separate: the traditional world of video games and the whimsical world of fantasy and adventure comics.

We see this same pattern repeat itself in other businesses and ventures. In each case, white space opens up an opportunity for an outsider to come in and to introduce ideas that had not been considered before.

That is exactly what happened with the birth of swing music. Born in Georgia, Fletcher Henderson moved to New York in 1920 to pursue a master's degree in chemistry from Columbia University. But Henderson soon realized that no one at the time would hire an African American chemist. So he turned to music, his first love, performing on the piano and eventually forming his own band, which attracted such luminaries as Louis Armstrong.

Throughout the 1920s Henderson's band performed in storied venues such as the Roseland Ballroom in midtown Manhattan and the Savoy Ballroom uptown in Harlem. Henderson was one of the top bandleaders in the city when the stock market crashed in 1929. Desperate for money, he looked to sell his most prized possession: his songbook.

Think about what would happen today if one of the era's most talented musicians were to sell off his repertoire of songs. You'd have a circus of people vying for rights. But in those days Henderson's music was largely unknown outside northern cities such as New York and Chicago. It took another relative outsider, the son of Russian Jewish immigrants, to recognize the true value of Henderson's songbook.

Born in Chicago in 1909, Benny Goodman enrolled in a music class at the local synagogue at the age of ten. As the northern terminus of trains coming up from the Mississippi delta, Goodman's Chicago was a hotbed for jazz and blues. African American musicians coming out of the South filled the air with their music.

When Goodman began playing with local orchestras in the 1920s, it was the swinging blues of the South that was being played in the clubs and dance halls. He moved to New York City in 1926, shortly after the death of his father. Always a shrewd businessman, Goodman survived the 1929 crash rather well. Hearing of Henderson's financial woes, he wanted to help his fellow musician—as well as cash in on a lucrative investment opportunity.

Over the next few years Goodman built a repertoire

out of Henderson's songs. In 1934, Goodman's ensemble got a gig as the house band on the national radio show *Let's Dance*, and Henderson's music was finally getting exposure.

Because the band performed live at midnight, however, few people were actually awake to listen to it, as became painfully evident when the band went on tour. As it toured the East Coast, in city after city Goodman's band found itself playing to half-empty halls.

But that all changed one August night when Goodman traveled out west to Oakland, California, for a gig at McFadden's Ballroom.

When Goodman pulled out Henderson's arrangements, the full house at McFadden's went wild. Luckily for Goodman—and for swing—this was not a freak event. The same thing happened two nights later in Los Angeles at the Palomar Ballroom: a full house and eager, enthusiastic dancers.

Why was Goodman's music so well received in California? *Let's Dance* was broadcast live across the nation at midnight Eastern time. While most people on the East Coast were sleeping then, the West Coast kids were wide awake and listening—it was only nine o'clock. They loved the new music and could hardly get enough of it. The swing era was under way, and Benny Goodman would be crowned its king.

Granted, Benny Goodman had plenty of talent of

his own. He was an excellent performer and a keen interpreter of good music. But what made Benny Goodman different was how he acted as an intermediator for, a translator of, African American music in American popular culture.

As a member of an immigrant community, Goodman began outside mainstream American culture himself. This made him less likely to adhere to cultural norms and the "proper" ways of performing. He transgressed racial and musical boundaries and translated between the white and black worlds. Goodman's background made him comfortable in the African American community, while the fact that he was white gave him an entree into traditional white music establishments. He was able to weave together two worlds.

Renegades or unusual suspects such as Goodman and Kary Mullis help to introduce, merge, and mix ideas from disparate spheres and spread them throughout a culture, society, or organization—just as the humanists at the dawn of the Renaissance introduced new ideas within the Catholic Church.

Cardinal Nicholas of Cusa, for example, in the fifteenth century, was a man of science. The notion of a cardinal being a scientist would have been laughable a century earlier. And yet the cardinal ground his own eyeglasses so that he could continue to read despite his myopia. On a trip across the Mediterranean Sea, he imagined that perhaps the earth was not at the center of the universe. His thoughts on the world would influence Copernicus and Kepler. His works in mathematics influenced Leibniz in his invention of calculus.

Inviting In the Unusual Suspect

At Cisco Systems, Ron Ricci, vice president of corporate positioning, embraced the notion of inviting in unusual suspects within a large tech company that is decidedly practical. Ricci points out that in many organizations, employees hitch their careers to their managers and try to take a vertical ride up through the organizational ranks on the heels of their boss. As Ricci sees it, there are two problems with this. The first is that it creates silos of loyalty—employees who are loyal to their boss and not to the company as a whole. The second is that employees may not be doing what they are best at or happiest doing, but in order to stay on the vertical ride, they don't explore other options.

To counter this, Ricci has encouraged a system of "lateral flow" at Cisco. Cisco actually encourages employees to move around the company, to try out different jobs in different departments with different responsibilities. This lateral flow of employees invites in unusual suspects.

People who start their careers in finance may end up in sales; others who start out in human resources may end up in customer service.

Dave Holland, for example, began his career at Cisco in real estate. A company like Cisco, with tens of thousands of employees, needs a lot of land for its multiple campuses. So when the Oakland A's were looking to unload a piece of land, they began conversations with Dave Holland about Cisco acquiring it.

During the negotiations, however, Holland recognized an opportunity for Cisco to offer technology inside sports stadiums. Real estate and professional sports are two worlds that would rarely intersect. But Cisco had been consciously organized to be responsive to ideas like the ones Dave Holland presented.

Among these ideas was to offer technologies to manage the content displayed on the video screens across the stadium, from the jumbo screen atop the scoreboard to the small ones at the hot dog stands.

Typically a company would hand such a project over to someone more experienced with Cisco's technology. Instead, Cisco put Dave Holland in charge of the new venture.

By allowing its employees to move from one department to another, Cisco creates the opportunity for an unusual suspect to come up with an entirely new business. The challenge, of course, is that allowing an unusual suspect to enter the scene is one thing, and listening to him or her is entirely another.

The army found this out the hard way.

In 2003 Americans were watching reports from Afghanistan and Iraq and wondering why things were going wrong. Coming out of retirement to become chief of staff of the U.S. Army, General Peter Schoomaker ordered a report on lessons learned. The report came to some interesting, if sobering, conclusions.

The army had suffered from groupthink, taking a dogged, American-centric viewpoint and failing to hear alternative voices. Many leaders in the army and among the civilian ranks of the Department of Defense imagined themselves as the cavalry in an old Hollywood western, riding in to the sound of a bugle to save the day. They convinced themselves that the Iraqis would be waiting with open arms when the United States invaded their country. What was tragic was that there *were* dissenting voices, but as an institution the army wasn't able to listen to them.

"The problem with our modern wars," General Dempsey explained to me, "is that you have privates on the ground who realize we're fighting a different war.

They see it every day. And they're adjusting. And then you have the general officers. And I think many of us are realizing that the way the army will look in twenty years is very, very different from how it looks today.

"But then you have the people in the middle. The majors, the lieutenant colonels. They've been with the organization for ten, fifteen, twenty years. And they don't want to change. They want to keep doing their job. And they realize that I'm not going to be there in two years. So they 'yes, sir' me, knowing full well that they can just wait me out."

Enter our friend Steve Rotkoff, who was one of the founding members of Red Team University, which strove to create critical thinkers, giving officers both the tools to become productive dissenters and the platform to offer their viewpoints.

Students in the university were challenged to think in new ways, to learn to see a problem from multiple perspectives. It was often an uphill battle in an organization that prided itself more on physical fitness and unswerving loyalty than on teasing out the many different ways of looking at a problem.

"You know," Steve once told me, "one of the things I found most frustrating during my service was that some elements of the army ridicule intellectualism. The army is so much about 'doing something to fix the problem' that it sometimes diminishes the importance of thinking deeply about the problem as well. The Red Team idea is about doing both, better."

The Army Liberates . . . Itself

"You know," Steve reminded me for the fourth time that day, "I'm the guardian of government resources, and I take that job very seriously." I nodded and gave him an appreciative look, trying to reassure him that I wasn't attempting to rip off Uncle Sam. I had suggested that the army could learn a lot by visiting Albert Einstein Medical Center in Philadelphia. This was one of the hospitals where Lisa Kimball and her nonprofit, the Plexus Institute, were using a process called liberating structures to fight MRSA. (Remember the janitor and the hot water?)

"You're looking at me and nodding," Steve continued, "but here I am in a goddamned hospital. Why are you going to drag a bunch of officers to visit a hospital? And why the hell would you spend government resources, precious resources, so they can learn how nurses are washing their hands?"

I pointed out to Steve that a hospital is a lot like the army. It's very hierarchical, with doctors on top. The staff wears uniforms. And hospitals contain highly siloed departments.

What was interesting about the hospital was that it had brought rather disparate voices into the conversation about controlling MRSA infection. And the results were stunning: MRSA rates had dropped by nearly half. Something was going on that wasn't pure serendipity. So I'd invited Steve to come take a look.

Our cab drove past the University of Pennsylvania and then a series of abandoned warehouses. We were clearly in an economically depressed part of town. The staff members who greeted us at Albert Einstein Medical Center, however, were warm and welcoming.

"We're so glad that the army is visiting," a nurse told us, echoing a sentiment I've often heard since. "We just don't have interaction with the armed services, and it's so encouraging, especially with all the news, that there are positive things going on."

Our host, along with Lisa Kimball, was Dr. Jeff Cohn, who at the time was the chief quality officer at the hospital. The white-haired physician explained that hospital-acquired infections had become such a problem that the institution needed to do *something* different to stop all these preventable deaths.

After a tour of the hospital (where I couldn't help but douse my hands with sanitizer at every doorway), we were invited to have orange juice and bagels and sit in on a group meeting.

"You're bringing me to a meeting?" Steve started to

fume. "You know how many meetings I see every day? Why do we need to sit in on another meeting?" At the meeting, people from different departments shared how things were going and how each of them was feeling. You could almost see the steam coming out of Steve's ears.

At the end, one of the nurses asked me, "What did you think?" I tried to make nice and reflected on the power of teams. Steve stayed silent.

"Are we going home now?" he finally asked me. Then the same nurse invited us to a small breakout session.

"This is the huddle for the nurse technicians," she explained with a warm smile. Steve, ever gracious, agreed to stay. And that's when things changed.

All five women in the breakout group were on the lower rungs of the hospital's hierarchy. They hadn't received much formal education, and their jobs were some of the toughest in the hospital—washing patients and changing sheets.

One of the nurse techs immediately spoke up. "I want to bring something up. Is that okay?"

"Sure," the facilitator said.

"Well, something's been bugging me. And I've been trying to let it go and shut my big mouth"—at this, the other women laughed—"but I can't. I work in the MRSA isolation unit. And it's a double room. So I get one patient who has a serious infection, but the other patient, he seems almost fine. Sure, he tested positive for MRSA, but his skin isn't covered with sores. And it just worries me. What if we're *infecting* the patient who isn't as sick?" The other techs nodded in unison.

"That is messed up!" one of them chimed in.

I expected the facilitator to quiet the protest, or at best suggest that perhaps she'd bring up the matter in a future staff meeting. Instead, she got on the phone with Dr. Cohn.

Five minutes later, Dr. Cohn was in the room with us, listening to the concern. "I had no idea this was happening," he said. "This wasn't a decision made by infection control. And you're right, we should change the policy." And with that, the change was made.

"Unbelievable!" said Steve, who up to this point had remained silent. He went on, "This is *unbelievable*. You just fixed a huge problem. You just saved lives." He started laughing. "And the knowledge was there all along. You just had to get the right people in the same room."

Dr. Cohn explained to him, "This happens every day. In hospitals these are people who never have much of a voice. And we found that we just have to . . ." He paused. "We have to listen. Because the knowledge, as you say, is there."

And that's when the light went on for Steve and me. We didn't just need to have dissenters in the army; we

needed to teach people to intermediate between different worlds, even in an organization with the rigidity and
structure of the army.

Thus, among the tasks of Red Team University is
teaching soldiers and officers alike to become like Lisa,
acting as weavers, intermediaries, in whatever big or
small way they can. One soldier said something that, for
me, captured it all: "I thought my job as a leader was
to come into a unit and tell people what to do. To be a
mentor and a guide, but also to take charge. Now I realize
my job is to draw out ideas, to listen, and to connect."

(6)

ACCELERATING SERENDIPITY

A year after I met him, General Dempsey was diagnosed with throat cancer. After what must have been a painful treatment program, he was making a recovery.

I was used to fast-paced meetings with him where we jumped from one topic to the other. But this time, on one of his first days back to the office, there was a quietness and stillness to our conversation. "You look well," I said. "I imagine you've been through a lot. Has your experience battling cancer changed you, do you think?"

"Well, of course, it's made me take stock of my life. And it made me realize I'm not immortal. But mostly it taught me to listen. I don't think I listened as well before the cancer. The irony, of course, is that the treatment has damaged my ears, so I need to concentrate even more."

Just then his aide entered, carrying a bowl of clam chowder for the general. Looking at me, the general said, "I couldn't find anything—what's that word?—vegan for you. But I had them make you a salad."

"Thank you. We seem like such opposites in so many ways," I said to him. "I suspect that not many people would envision us sitting down together this way."

"That's the nice thing about serendipity," he replied. And indeed it was serendipity that had first brought us together. General Dempsey had become aware of my work in a roundabout fashion, when an army officer picked up my first book. It eventually made its way to General Stanley McChrystal, who was in charge of U.S. forces in Afghanistan. From there the book continued to circulate through the Pentagon and eventually landed in General Dempsey's lap. He had been intrigued by some of the ideas in it.

As I ate my salad, I realized there was no way I could have predicted our working together. It wasn't as if I had sat down and mapped out a plan to introduce myself to the man who would become chairman of the Joint Chiefs of Staff. But, knowing what I knew about white space and unusual suspects, it was clear to me that chaos had played a role in our meeting. In shaping future events, there's planning and there's luck. But there's also something in between, I believe: *setting the conditions for serendipity to occur.*

Serendipity at Stanford

Marie Mookini was easily the person most beloved by the student body at Stanford's Graduate School of Business (GSB). That's because, as head of admissions for ten years, Marie was responsible for letting students *in*. Each acceptance letter had a handwritten note signed by her, letting the applicant know why he or she had been selected.

"The old admissions model," she said, "was that you wanted all of your students to be well rounded. Every student coming in should be skilled at math and English and music and science." It makes sense that a university would want candidates who don't just perform well on standardized tests but also have a solid academic background.

Marie realized, however, that simply having a well-rounded class wasn't sufficient. "Over the past two decades," she continued, "that model has shifted. Today's model celebrates differences. Each student admitted has a special texture, a special angle. The students serve to make each other better."

In a way, you could argue that Marie had an easy task

working at Stanford, one of the top schools in the country: she got to select from a very bright group of applicants who had done well as undergraduates and succeeded in their jobs. But at the same time, Marie was entrusted with a huge responsibility: how could she construct an incoming class such that the students would make one another better? It turns out that, like Lisa Kimball in the hospital, an important part of Marie's job was to create the right environment for serendipity to occur.

One of Marie's hires to the admissions committee was Allison Rouse, a lifelong friend of Judah Pollack, my co-author on this book, so we turned to him for an up-close perspective on how the committee makes its decisions. Allison grew up in the projects in the South Bronx. After attending the University of Pennsylvania, he took a job working at Penn in undergraduate admissions and eventually became a gatekeeper to one of the country's premier business schools.

"About 50 to 60 percent of the class, give or take," Allison explains, "is going to be made up of people who are an academic force and who are also nice. These are low-risk people. They're going to get in and they're going to do well. They're liberal arts people who graduated and went to work for Goldman Sachs, an investment bank, or a consulting firm."

This group tends to apply to Stanford after two to four years in the workforce. What they have in common is quantitative skills. They all have solid business fundamentals, be it crunching numbers and analyzing data or knowing how to ask the right questions and apply the answers to the appropriate situation. We'll call this first group the shoo-ins. They hail from schools such as Stanford, Harvard, Princeton, Penn, Dartmouth, and UC Berkeley. They are top-tier students who can do the work.

Another important part of the class, anywhere from 5 to 15 percent, is what Allison and Marie refer to as "uniquely talented people": individuals who have excelled at something, though not necessarily academics. Members of this group did well in school, but they weren't necessarily the valedictorians. Their GMAT scores were okay, but they didn't ace the test. What these uniquely talented people do have going for them is an extraordinary ability, such as being a world-renowned classical violinist, an Olympic swimmer, or a physics genius.

At one orientation Marie told the new incoming class, "You have some extraordinary people here, including a former NASA employee, a rocket scientist. And she's awesome." The class broke out in applause.

The third category, accounting for 25 percent or so, adds to the diversity of the class. They're not only smart and qualified but also come from diverse cultures, ethnicities, religions, and regions of the world. "You want people to realize that they're not that different," Allison says. "People tend to hire people who look like them, who act like them. We want them to get comfortable with more different people. That way there will be more different ideas in the room."

The fourth and last group is where things get really interesting. They bring a different kind of diversity: diversity of life experience. While they may not have excelled in the traditional way, they have often overcome significant challenges. I call this last group the "secret sauce" because they introduce zest and flavor to the student body.

Some "secret sauce" admits may have done military tours in Iraq and Afghanistan; one may be a manager at a steel mill; another may be raising a child as a single parent while holding down a demanding job. They often come from underrepresented industries, as opposed to the 50 to 60 percent of students who come directly out of the financial industry or consulting.

"These are the students that ground your class," Allison explains. "If you have a class of sixty people and they're reading a business case about a big company taking over a small company and you are asked to decide what to do as the small company's CEO, having someone in the class who has worked for a small company and understands what happens inside of one is going to change how the other students see the situation."

I remember, for example, during one of the first weeks

of classes, one of the professors presenting a case describing how Shell Oil responded to a Greenpeace protest campaign against its operations. The environmental organization was known for using small, highly maneuverable, inflatable boats to stop a whaling ship or disrupt a country's military from conducting underwater nuclear tests. When the class discussion turned to these boats, a retired navy officer muttered, "Those boats were a freaking pain in the ass." Everyone around her burst into laughter.

"Were you saying something?" the professor asked, looking at her.

"I was on a ship that had to deal with these protesters." She went on to describe exactly what it was like to be in that situation: Greenpeace boats zipping around your ship, you as a naval officer needing to decide how to respond.

This type of unlikely perspective is useful well beyond the classroom. Explains Allison, "If you have a class on union negotiation and you have the manager of a steel mill in there, that person is going to have a different perspective on the discussion than someone who came from Goldman Sachs. The steel mill manager will have real experience dealing with unions and workers who belong to unions. And because they're classmates they will be a part of each other's future network, which means their network is more diversified."

Indeed, the serendipity went well beyond classroom discussions. There are countless stories of students meeting in class or over pizza and deciding to start a new project or launch a company. You're reading this book because I happened to go on a backpacking trip with a woman from my class who happened to have gone to college with another classmate whose background was in banking and who used to live in Prague. He connected me to an older alum who had a passion for the environment and with whom I started a nonprofit, which led to my writing my first book, which was eventually picked up by General Dempsey. Talk about serendipity.

There is one final characteristic that applies to all the students, however.

"In admissions," says Allison, "you have to be aware that you're not building a class, you're building a community. I want kind people, helpful people. Will they be good alums? Will they be good community members? Will they be a good cultural fit? It gets to values. I can't train you in values. None of us can. We want people who want the responsibility of being a part of a community."

If you come from a privileged economic or academic background, for example, the admissions team is looking to see that you have some self-reflection about your privilege.

"When I read that someone is 'extremely hardworking' and that alone, that is not a good thing," Allison says. "Where are the other qualities? I want to hear that you're hardworking but also that you make other people better, that you help others."

In undergraduate admissions, admissions officers look for a certain number of students who will "bleed the school colors"— students who feel that being a part of the school community, being an engaged alum, is one of the reasons they want to come to the school. At Stanford's GSB, the admissions team looks for the same thing. They want students who value the school, their class, and their classmates. They attempt to create an environment that exposes students to different types of excellence from different parts of the world and different parts of society. They try to ensure that their students value one another's opinions, experiences, and points of view. They consciously work to build a community that is reflective and kind.

And it is by organizing around those values that they inspire serendipity. The interesting thing about this process is that variations of it are taking place across a variety of fields. While the goals might be different, the paths toward serendipity are similar.

The Anatomy of a Dinner Party

Robin Starbuck Farmanfarmaian has an easy smile and long blond ringlets of hair, and she may stretch to five feet five inches . . . if she's wearing four-inch heels. She sits on the board of the San Francisco Ballet and has chaired its gala for the past four years. She is also a master of throwing the perfect dinner party.

From that description most people would assume that she provides good food, hosts in welcoming environments, and invites interesting people. She does indeed do all of that, in much the same way that admissions committee members look at GPAs and test scores. But there's a whole lot more to planning a successful dinner party, according to Robin. She thinks of a dinner party as an opportunity to create serendipity. "All good hosts know that every party that goes well has an element of serendipity to it," she says. "That's the joy. But that doesn't mean you can't organize things beforehand to greatly improve your odds."

Over brunch, we tried to find out her secret to doing just that—improving the odds. She started by telling us things that made us appreciate just how much goes into throwing the perfect event: taking care of guests' needs, keeping the conversation moving, even finding the perfect lighting. "If I wanted this to be a more formal event," she said, using our meal as an example,

"I would light candles, dim the chandelier, put on soft background music."

It's this very caring approach that makes guests feel welcome. But the three strategies she revealed next were actually rather surprising.

First, regardless of the size of the event, the location, or whether it is formal or informal, Robin always considers what the *goal* of the party is. It sounds counterintuitive—we expect serendipity to just emerge, right?

"It's the first thing I ask myself: what is the goal of the party?" she explained. Remember that planned serendipity lies somewhere between the control of a highly managed event and random chance. There are things we can do to nudge serendipity along. At one dinner party, Robin continued, "the goal was to have a good time. Other times the goal could be to facilitate a business opportunity for a guest or myself, or to create buzz around a charity event, or to talk about the future of health care."

Having a goal is very different from having an agenda. You want to focus people without constraining them, something that is equally true in a corporate environment. "Whenever you bring a group of people together, the key to making it work is to set and meet expectations," she says. "That is how you drive happiness."

The second strategy Robin revealed is nuanced but

very important. Rather than just worrying about the things that will *foster* serendipity, it's important to prevent those things that will *detract* from it. "You don't want an entire room full of introverts," she said, listing the things she'd worry about. "You need two or three extroverted people to keep things going." Robin adds that it's important to think about whether any of the potential guests might not get along—"unless it's entertaining to watch them fight," she joked. "Even if they don't fight out loud, people will feel something is wrong, but they won't know why. No amount of hosting can fix that."

You want to make people feel comfortable, she says. An example is "making sure everyone knows how to dress, that everyone is dressed in the same general way." Robin might be direct and tell a man to wear a suit or be more subtle and tell a woman what she herself is going to wear. "If someone shows up in jeans and sneakers but everyone else is in cocktail dresses, the guest in jeans may feel ill at ease."

The third strategy involves getting help when you are inevitably pulled away to attend to other matters. "I'm a very good host," she affirms, "but some hosting responsibilities are naturally going to take me away from the party—things like checking on dinner, answering the door, putting a jacket on the bed, or having a private conversation with one of my guests." So it is absolutely necessary, she says, to invite a second host, someone who is extremely extroverted and skilled at conversation. "A good host knows how to drive a conversation."

But if you think that this is how Robin spends her days, planning dinner parties, you'd be wrong. She's the vice president of strategic relations at Singularity University.

Singularity is not a university in the traditional sense. Its mission is to educate business and political leaders about technologies that are growing at an exponential rate. It incubates projects that may seem as if they came out of the pages of a science fiction book: computer-driven cars, nanobots that keep patients healthy, and unmanned aerial vehicles that distribute supplies to people in inaccessible areas of the world.

At Singularity, Robin applies the same strategies that she uses to create successful dinner parties to ensure that the visits of CEOs and political leaders are as fruitful as possible. "It's my job to build the relationships, increase engagement, and to create an environment where serendipity can take form."

Serendipity and the *Huffington Post*

It was the kind of gathering that would make gossip reporters and paparazzi drool. The crowd of thirty or so people was eclectic: actress Meg Ryan, studio mogul David Geffen, comedian Larry David, *West Wing* creator Aaron Sorkin, and Democratic political consultants Peter Daou and James Boyce. You'd think it was a movie launch, or an after-party for the Oscars. But this was a group with a mission: to change the landscape of American politics.

What's interesting is just how wildly successful the results were.

The type of gathering I'm describing has a long lineage that dates back to pre-revolution France and the original social form of planned serendipity: the French salon.

Eighteenth-century salons drew their name from the receiving room used by the lady of a French château. Being on the woman's side of the house, these chambers were, by their very nature, not where official political power resided, as that rested with the lord or king. But these gatherings held in these spaces offered a more open, fluid atmosphere and attracted intellectuals, artists, politicians, and the wealthy, who came to discuss cultural happenings. Rousseau or Voltaire might discuss the nature of man and the possibility of a fair government while powerful and influential people in attendance listened and took heed.

These salons rarely had a specific agenda or goal. They were designed around people with common interests coming together and talking. Despite their inconsequential appearance (an informal place where people could engage in intellectual, unstructured conversation), the salons followed a powerful recipe that's by now familiar to us. Salons offered eighteenth-century society the white space of having no agenda; functioning outside the official structures of French power, they invited unusual suspects. And the results, as we have come to expect, were surprising.

The stories and ideas of the American Revolution were shared in the salons of Paris, stirring the population in a way that ultimately exploded into the French Revolution. In the years to follow, the ideals of women's suffrage and modernism were discussed, with equally large-scale effect on broader society.

And this brings us back to the present day and the gathering that took place on December 3, 2004, in Los Angeles.

Seven decades earlier, in the 1930s, Los Angeles was awash in European intellectuals who had fled Europe's growing Fascism. One of the things they brought with them was the concept of the salon.

Paul Holdengräber, the head of the Institute for Art and Cultures at the Los Angeles County Museum of Art, says of modern-day Los Angeles, "This is a particularly discombobulated city, a city with no real center. People want to have a place to share the life of the mind."

Thus the salon became a lasting meme of sorts in Los Angeles, with various luminaries over the years hosting their own.

Anaïs Nin, the French writer and memoirist, ran the Garden of Allah salon (in the Silver Lake area of Los Angeles), whose members included authors Raymond Chandler and F. Scott Fitzgerald and playwright Bertolt Brecht. Writer Thomas Mann was a frequent guest at one salon; Aldous Huxley held his own.

More recently, Arianna Huffington threw coveted book salons. "There are many L.A.'s," Huffington said. "And one thing these book parties do is bring the L.A.'s together." Often attended by Hollywood's elite, the parties were mostly about people coming together to talk. But when you bring people from different backgrounds and different walks of life together, any number of creative ideas can emerge.

A month after John Kerry suffered a stinging defeat in the 2004 presidential election, many powerful Democrats, dismayed, wanted to do something. Huffington, who had been running her book salons for years, called a meeting at her house early that December. Although she chose her guest list with great care, following the serendipitous nature of salons, the gathering had no specific agenda. But, as at Robin Farmanfarmaian's parties, there *was* a goal: to take back the White House. More specifically, the goal was to find a way to offer a liberal response to the *Drudge Report,* an influential conservative online publication.

What emerged from that salon was the *Huffington Post.*

It's important to note that many of the people at Arianna Huffington's house that night in December 2004 were renegades; they weren't the people you'd expect to find in a room where strategic political decisions are being made. Politics was not their area of expertise or influence. What brought them together was the same thing that Marie Mookini and Allison Rouse look for in MBA applicants—a commitment to community, in this case, a Hollywood community interested in changing the prevailing political winds.

Arianna Huffington's outreach to celebrities might seem a little ostentatious. But one of the things that drew readers to the *Huffington Post* in its early years was its use of celebrity blogging. And the *Huffington Post* has been a potent publication emphasizing perspectives of the left ever since.

Serendipity and the Organizational Silo

As we've seen time and again, serendipity depends on the flow of ideas and the intermingling of unlikely people. Organizational silos are the enemy of serendipity: it's hard to find serendipity isolated in a cubicle.

I don't think I had a full appreciation of just how compartmentalized organizations can be until one night during my army program when I was sitting in a bar in Augusta with a group of officers on their third round of beers. Things were getting jovial as they exchanged funny stories about kids and army life.

"Wait a second," a guy named Chip said, turning to another officer named Dan, who had just finished a story about a recent assignment. "Which building do you work in?" Chip and Dan were stationed in the same army post. They had exchanged several emails in the past to coordinate on a project but had never met in person.

"I work in building 133. How about you?"

"No kidding? Are you serious?" They worked in the same building. Chip couldn't believe it. "Which floor?" It turned out that not only did the two work in the same building, but their cubicles were only ten yards away from each other. And yet they had never actually *met* until they came here to Augusta.

"That's just so whacked," said Chip. "Someone can

be sitting right there next to us, and instead of going over and talking, we'll just send an email."

Institutions across a variety of sectors are recognizing that increased use of email and a walled-off cubicle environment lead to separation and isolation. Recognizing this simple yet sobering truth, organizations have tried various approaches to break through the silos, from brown-bag lunches to office socials. But breaking silos isn't easy.

"What happens in these things is torturous," reflected Chip. "You just stand and talk with the people you already know."

"You know, there's a *name* we have for those kinds of functions," chimed in Dan. "Mandatory fun."

The problem with mandatory fun is that while we can attempt to nudge serendipity, it's hard to force it. The army used to have officers' clubs, where officers would eat, mingle, and have a couple of drinks.

The importance of alcohol in military culture is that there is an unwritten rule that while drinking together, you can speak to other officers—even superiors—in a nonattribution manner—the conversation is "off the record." Let's say, for example, that a senior officer gives you an order that is legal and ethical but happens to be nonstrategic or misguided. Your job is to follow the order out of respect for the hierarchy. At the officers' club, however, over a drink, you can speak your mind, and the worst-case scenario is that the next day you feign that you had too much to drink. The white space created by being able to say what you're really thinking allows unusual suspects (i.e., very junior officers or people from other parts of the unit) to break down silos.

But alcohol consumption, of course, has a price. Drinking leads to intoxication and to driving under the influence. Moreover, the mostly male clubs were often seen as sexist and sometimes even antagonistic to women. Over the years, officers' clubs have disappeared. And brown-bag lunches just don't offer the same opportunity for serendipity and the breakdown of social barriers.

So what can we do? Remember Robin Farman-farmaian's second rule of dinner parties: remove the *obstacles* to serendipity. Two approaches being used by organizations are especially interesting for our purposes: The first is a technology-dependent approach that creates small yet very effective siphons between the various departmental silos of a company. The second seeks to completely reimagine the physical nature of an office.

Companies like Microsoft's Yammer, Salesforce's Chatter, and Jive all recognize that social networks like Facebook and Twitter are highly effective at fostering serendipity. People can connect with friends or friends of friends to find housing, new jobs, or even new friends. The problem is that you don't want employees to post internal company issues on a public forum like Facebook.

The idea, then, was to come up with an enterprise social network—that is, a Facebook-like platform (some might say clone) that is internal to the organization. Users can post pictures, write updates, and even follow one another on a stream, much as you might follow Justin Bieber on Twitter.

The results were surprising: unlike other would-be collaboration tools, people actually used these networks. In Sydney, Australia, a second-year consultant for the accounting firm Deloitte Australia, for example, had come up with an innovative solution to a problem faced by one of the agency's big clients. But he wasn't sure if it would work. More to the point, he wasn't sure if the client would find the solution as innovative as he did.

In a Hollywood movie, we'd have our consultant stumble into the CEO in the elevator or share a taxi with the senior partner who handled the client—some random, serendipitous event that led to his being able to share his idea with the right person. What the consultant actually did, however, although not as dramatic, was far more effective—he posted his question on Deloitte Australia's enterprise activity stream, in much the same way Justin Bieber might tweet about his new tour.

A partner in risk services, based in Melbourne, saw the posting and suggested that the young consultant talk to one of two partners in Deloitte for help. An hour later the head of consulting chimed in. He said that he knew both of the partners in question and that one of them was the better one to talk to. Armed with the recommendation of the head of consulting, the second-year consultant called the suggested partner the next morning and got the feedback he needed.

Imagine if your company, your school, your agency, had a social media platform analogous to Facebook that was private, accessible only to people affiliated with your group. People could reach out to one another, comment on one another's ideas and suggestions, and make new connections. Your name is associated with your posting, but not your title, your level of seniority, or what you do. A second-year consultant with a good idea can get feedback from the head of consulting. Information flows. Serendipity accelerates.

Essentially, this kind of enterprise activity stream is an exchange forum that enables information on the fringes of an organization to be seen and heard.

Indeed, if information is on the fringe, you want to have as much interchange among people as possible to encourage communication—to remove the barriers to one person talking to another. A sea of cubicles in which hierarchy rules kills this opportunity.

In response, some companies have turned to so-called open offices, tearing down the cubicles and leaving vast areas without walls and with open tables for people to work at. Employees in these firms don't have an assigned place—they must find a new spot, or stake out their old one, each day. The idea is that one day you might work at this table, another at a different one, and in the process you'll interact with a great many more colleagues. In some firms, employees have lockers—just as in high school—where they keep personal effects (pictures, coffee mugs, candies) to put on their table.

The problem with this approach, however, is that it's *too* unstructured. Employees feel unmoored and respond to the open office by buying powerful noise-canceling headphones, which, obviously, defeats the purpose of fostering the serendipitous exchange of information.

This is why New York mayor Michael Bloomberg might be on to something. When he was first elected, he decided to ditch the mayor's traditional office and instead moved into the Board of Estimate chamber on the second floor of City Hall, where he ordered all the walls knocked down. As mayor, he shared his office with fifty-one other city officials. His desk was the same size as everyone else's, and Bloomberg sat in the middle, with his first deputy mayor an arm's length away. The space is known as Bloomberg's "bullpen."

Bloomberg imported the idea from his days at Salomon Brothers, where traders would share information throughout the day across their low cubicle dividers.

The mayor's bullpen is an open office, but it differs from most other such layouts in two important ways.

First of all, people are given a space to call their own, in which they can put up family pictures and other personal effects, but their space is in much closer proximity to their fellow workers.

Second, Bloomberg sits at the center. In other words, the boss is *right there* in the middle of things, holding people accountable by his presence, staying abreast of what is happening, and remaining accessible to his team of direct reports as well as to those five rungs down the hierarchy. Bloomberg holds important meetings out in the open. Others in the room see the meetings going on and can often hear what is being said.

At first a lot of City Hall employees were unhappy with the setup. One former worker said, "It is something that you do not think that you can ever get used to. But when you see the mayor hosting high-level meetings in clear sight of everyone else, you start to understand that this open-communication model is not bullshit. And that it works."

Ed Skyler, the deputy mayor for administration, said that the mayor likes the setup because "it really catalyzes the flow of information." According to Bloomberg, the openness encourages people to approach him with their ideas and questions who might not ordinarily do so because of the typical office obstacles of long corridors, closed doors, secretaries, and deputies.

Washington, D.C.'s former mayor, Adrian Fenty, a Bloomberg mentee, used the bullpen layout as well. His legislative chief, Joanne Ginsburg, said, "In the time it would take to send five emails back and forth to talk about a situation, you can solve it with a short conversation."

The bullpen allows for a greater flow of information and for more serendipitous events to occur. As Bloomberg said, "I issue proclamations telling everyone to work together, but it's the lack of walls that really makes them do it."

And that's the nice thing about creating an environment that fosters serendipity. With a little bit of white space and the ability to interact with others who are different, amazing, and serendipitous, things tend to happen.

(7)

PUTTING IT ALL TOGETHER: CHAOS AND SILICON VALLEY

The Mystery of the Valley

Being in Robert Swanson's shoes as he was about to meet Dr. Herbert Boyer would have made most of us cringe in the way we do when we know someone has virtually zero interest in hearing from us.

It was 1973, and Dr. Boyer, a researcher at the University of California at San Francisco medical school, was conducting research that was gaining international attention. He had developed a way to combine pieces of DNA from two different species and make a new DNA strand. This was rather significant, because if you could reintroduce the new DNA strand back into a cell, this new modified cell could be trained to fight a disease or to act as a specialized vaccine.

Robert Swanson, meanwhile, was just twenty-nine and worked for what was then a small, upstart venture capital firm called Kleiner Perkins. His goal was to convince Boyer that the research on DNA was an excellent foundation on which to build a new company. Dr. Boyer had no idea why a young kid from a technology-oriented venture capital firm in the heart of Silicon Valley would want to talk to a biochemist. He was so uninterested in meeting Swanson that he gave him only ten minutes.

But Swanson must have been convincing. The ten-minute meeting stretched to three hours, and at the end of it Dr. Boyer agreed to let Kleiner Perkins back a new venture they called Genentech. Within two years Genentech had figured out how to synthesize insulin in the laboratory and in doing so invented the industry known as biotechnology.

Why is it that Silicon Valley, named for the key element used in its signature industry, microchips, continues to invent new industries to this day? More specifically, why is it that Silicon Valley is able to consistently accomplish this, while other cities and regions throughout the world can't?

Almost no other region on earth has enjoyed such astounding resilience and creativity. The majority of the world's famous regions of production are identified with a single product or industry. Modena, Italy, is known for balsamic vinegar. Detroit is known as the Motor City for its car industry. Pittsburgh became famous for its steel. And Los Angeles is the entertainment capital of the world, where movies are made.

While Hollywood still makes movies and Detroit still makes cars and Modena still makes balsamic vinegar, Silicon Valley has developed an economy based on much more than just silicon. It has become the center of biotechnology, medical technology, Internet technology, social networking, and the burgeoning field of green technology, as well as a hotbed of social entrepreneurship. The question, of course, is how.

Geniuses, Gold, and Lots of Money

There are three interesting theories that aim to explain Silicon Valley's uniqueness. The first two come to us from UC Berkeley professor AnnaLee Saxenian in her book *Regional Advantage: Culture and Competition in Silicon Valley and Route 128.*

Saxenian's first theory involves Silicon Valley's dense social network. If you put a lot of smart people in one place, they will start bumping into one another, talking, and interacting, and serendipitous things will emerge.

Entrepreneur Frank Levinson, for example, went to hear a presentation on endangered domestic animals. The dinner and presentation were hosted by Bob and Robyn Metcalfe. Bob was one of the legendary inventors of Ethernet technology. But Levinson wasn't invited because of business. He was invited because his preschool-age daughter loved cats and was friends with Metcalfe's daughter, who also loved cats.

At a later event, Metcalfe suggested that Levinson's company, Finisar, which was having trouble gaining a foothold in the fiber-optics industry, could be more appealing to the tech industry if it supported established industry standards. Levinson followed the advice and Finisar's fortunes took a turn for the better; Finisar became one of the leaders in fiber-optic solutions.

Silicon Valley's dense social network certainly explains at least some of the region's success. It's a magnet for entrepreneurs and tech geniuses, and if you put this many smart people together in one place, interesting and innovative things are likely to happen. But how does a region (or an organization) become such a magnet in the first place?

AnnaLee Saxenian's second theory has to do with a provision in the original Civil Code of California, enacted all the way back in 1872. The provision guaranteed employees in the state the right to choose their own place of work. Unlike companies in other states, California companies couldn't require their employees to sign noncompete clauses. That meant that an unhappy employee could leave his or her job and join a competitor, creating increased knowledge flow. The law has remained on the books over the decades, leading to some unintended and extremely beneficial consequences.

William Shockley, the co-inventor of the transistor at Bell Labs, moved to Mountain View, California, in 1956 to set up the eponymous Shockley Transistor Corporation. But Shockley was as famous for his inept management style as he was for his invention.

Once, for example, when trying to settle a rather inane office matter, he made everyone in the company take a lie detector test. But what really upset his young engineers was that Shockley gave up on silicon. Shockley's transistors were made from an element called germanium, which was easy to use but very expensive. Silicon, on the other hand, was plentiful and cheap. Furthermore, because of silicon's high melting point, transistors made from it continued to function at higher temperatures than those made from germanium. But processing silicon at the time was a challenge *because* of its high melting point. At first Shockley set out to make silicon practical, but then he killed the project.

At the time, most people tended to work for one company their whole lives, but eight of Shockley's brightest young engineers were fed up. Had it not been for the 1872 law barring noncompete clauses, they would have had only two options: either stay in the company or quit but have to work in a different industry sector. In California, however, they were able to start their own competing company, Fairchild Semiconductor, and Shockley couldn't do anything about it.

Fairchild Semiconductor figured out how to process silicon more easily and began using it to make transistors. One of the founding engineers was Eugene Kleiner, who would go on to co-found Kleiner Perkins, the venture capital firm that invested in Genentech. Another founder was Robert Noyce, who submitted a patent for an integrated circuit board made of silicon. After more than a decade with Fairchild, Noyce and fellow Fairchild engineer Gordon Moore broke away to start yet another company, Intel.

The trend continues today. What do Yammer, YouTube, Tesla Motors, and LinkedIn have in common? All are companies founded by former PayPal employees. People in Silicon Valley continue to move from company to company, bringing knowledge with them and encouraging the spirit of innovation and entrepreneurship.

From the viewpoint of organized chaos, dense social networks in the valley enable serendipity; the free movement of employees allows unusual suspects to move from company to company.

Still another theory about the rise of Silicon Valley is all about the money.

Fairchild Semiconductor got its name from an investor named Sherman Fairchild; a young MBA named Arthur Rock brokered the deal. Both were based in New York.

The East Coast money didn't allow for employee ownership. Having no stake in the company, however, ultimately led several engineers to break away from Fairchild and start their own ventures. Eventually Arthur Rock moved out west and started Silicon Valley's first major venture capital firm, which would go on to fund Intel and Apple.

Today, a short walk up Sand Hill Road in Menlo Park, California, demonstrates how important it is to be in Silicon Valley if you're looking for money.

Benchmark Capital, at 2480 Sand Hill Road, funded Instagram, Yelp, and Twitter. Walk up to 2750 Sand Hill and you'll find Kleiner Perkins, funders of Google, Intuit, AOL, Compaq, Symantec, VeriSign, Zynga, WebMD, and, of course, Genentech. Draper Fisher Jurvetson, a few doors down at 2882 Sand Hill, funded SolarCity, Hotmail, and Overture. Walk less than a mile from our original address to 3000 Sand Hill and you'll see the offices of Sequoia Capital, which invested in Google, YouTube, PayPal, Cisco Systems, Oracle, and Instagram.

But how and why did Silicon Valley attract so many smart people in the first place? Remember that when Silicon Valley was born, leaving one company to work for another was rather unusual, even in California. So what about Silicon Valley's culture made employees so comfortable jumping from job to job? And why is it that the venture capital firms are all based in the same location?

The answer to these questions involves the IQ test, tuberculosis, and the postwar military, as I first heard from Steve Blank, a professor of economics at Stanford, Columbia, and Harvard.

The Man Behind Silicon Valley

There's a real chance that Silicon Valley would never have become the legend it is today had it not been for the IQ test, or rather its inventor, Lewis Terman.

The psychologist took a professorship at Stanford University in 1910, bringing his ten-year-old son, Frederick, with him. Frederick Terman, in turn, grew up to earn his electrical engineering degree from Stanford. He went on to receive his PhD from MIT, and after receiving his doctorate, he was offered a job at the university. This gave Terman a free summer and the opportunity to travel. What was supposed to be a post-graduation trip back to his childhood home in Palo Alto,

however, would turn out to have life-threatening consequences.

During his visit to Palo Alto in 1924, Terman con-
tracted tuberculosis. There were no antibiotics to cure
the disease at the time, so instead of going back to MIT
to teach, Terman lay in bed with sandbags on his chest
to provide resistance and thereby strengthen his lungs.
Fortunately, Terman was able to make a recovery, and a
year after he fell ill, his former advisor at Stanford offered
him a part-time teaching position at the university.

It's important to note that back in those days, Stanford wasn't nearly the prestigious (and wealthy) school
that it is today. To give you a sense of the conditions
Terman taught in, when the Great Depression hit, the
roof of the electrical engineering department sprang a
leak, and with no money to fix it, the students built
wooden trays to catch the water. With no money to hire
new faculty, Terman encouraged his students to form
their own seminars and learn from one another.

From the get-go, Terman believed in loose control.
For example, instead of telling two of his students, Bill
Hewlett and David Packard, to stay in academia, he encouraged them to start their own company, which they
did, in a garage behind the house where Packard lived.

It was at Stanford that Terman would lay the founda-
tions for Silicon Valley. Not only would he make Stanford one of the best universities in the country, but he

would create white space for entrepreneurs to build new ventures and foster a community that welcomed unusual suspects.

It all began with the military. "You have to realize that before this was the Silicon Valley, for thirty years this was defense valley," Steve Blank told me. Blank, a college dropout, has been a part of eight start-ups in the valley, four of which went public. From the picturesque home he built on a bluff, the Pacific Ocean stretches across the horizon like a giant infinity pool. Silicon Valley has been very good to Blank.

Blank explained how when the United States entered World War II, President Franklin D. Roosevelt's chief science advisor, Vannevar Bush, recommended that the federal government start funding university labs directly by awarding them $450 million in defense contracts.

The result was a boon for academic institutions, or at least some of them.

MIT received $117 million to set up a secret lab that focused on improving radar technologies to enable the Allies to find enemy aircraft. Across the Charles River, meanwhile, Harvard got $30 million to set up its own secret lab and hired Professor Terman from Stanford to run it. This lab focused on developing radar-jamming technology to stop the Germans from locating Allied airplanes. MIT had no idea that Harvard's lab even existed: MIT researchers were baffled on a few occasions to discover that the radar in their lab wasn't working. Little did they know it was being unintentionally jammed by Terman's lab at Harvard.

Stanford, meanwhile, was left out of the picture. As millions were invested elsewhere, the school received a meager $50,000. Terman, who was used to leaking roofs, noted this huge discrepancy, which he was eager to address after the war when he returned to Stanford as dean of the engineering school. As luck would have it, he was able to turn to the man who had been his PhD advisor at MIT, none other than Vannevar Bush, FDR's science advisor.

Terman began by luring eleven engineers from his Harvard lab to start the Stanford Research Institute, or SRI. With the institute, Stanford received funding to develop microwave radar to track Soviet missiles.

Years later, when Terman was provost, the university was looking to expand its campus but was short on cash. When Leland Stanford had deeded his eight thousand acres to form the university, he had forbidden that any of the land ever be sold. But nothing in the deed said anything about renting. Terman offered long leases to companies to encourage them to establish locations near Stanford. He created the Stanford Research Park, which soon housed companies such as Eastman Kodak, General Electric, Lockheed, and his former students' Hewlett-Packard.

Terman's creation of SRI and the Research Park co-incided with the Korean War and the rise of the Soviet nuclear threat. By giving weapons developers the space they needed, the Research Park encouraged them to come to Palo Alto and partner with Stanford. And with the Soviet Union's launch of Sputnik, defense research money went into hyperdrive. The Small Business Investment Company was created to help launch new businesses, matching investments at a rate of three to one. Money began to flood into the valley.

Terman was a master at positioning Stanford to take advantage of defense spending. But that alone wouldn't have launched Silicon Valley. When the military doled out money to Stanford, it wanted the university to both develop *and* produce the technology. Terman, however, agreed only to conduct the research; he wanted the production to be done outside the school, by the companies located in Stanford Research Park.

Meanwhile, Terman himself was becoming more and more interwoven with the valley. Explained Steve Blank, "By the late 1950s Terman is sitting on the CIA's advisory board. He's on the advisory board for the army and the navy. The first three companies to go public, he's sitting on the boards of all three of them. Terman was a one-man venture capital industry."

White Space in Silicon Valley

As federal money started to flow into Stanford in the 1950s, Terman encouraged some of his graduate students to forget about continuing their PhD programs and instead start their own companies.

Such advice from a dean would have been unheard of in the Northeast. But the West Coast was culturally younger. It was easier for Terman to upend tradition at Stanford because there was less of it. At the time, Harvard was over three hundred years old, while Stanford was barely seventy-five. There were few powerful alumni to upset and fewer established ways of doing things. In the East, however, you went to college to get a degree so you could get a good job at IBM, GE, Westinghouse— the giants of the day. No one went to school, let alone dropped out, so that they could start their own company.

Today, regardless of which college they went to, every college student who has dropped out of school to start their own business since—from Steve Jobs to Bill Gates, from Larry Ellison to Mark Zuckerberg—was able to do so in part because Frederick Terman made it an acceptable part of the technology culture.

Throughout the Cold War, Stanford's engineering department did advanced research and development for the Central Intelligence Agency and the National

Security Agency, but it was the students and their start-ups that built the systems. In an effort to streamline the export of a new development from the Stanford lab that developed it to the start-up that would produce it, Terman eased the transfer of intellectual property. It took all of a few minutes to take what you were working on at Stanford, obtain the rights to it, and leave to start your own company.

Were it not for Terman's lenient intellectual property policies, Sergey Brin and Larry Page would have never been able to drop out of their PhD programs at Stanford to found Google. Sandra Lerner and Leonard Bosack wouldn't have been able to quit their staff positions to start Cisco. And Vinod Khosla and Scott McNealy wouldn't have been able to join fellow graduate student Andy Bechtolsheim in creating Sun Microsystems. Sun's original workstation, the product the company was founded on, was originally designed for Stanford's network and was built with parts from the university's computer science department.

While still at Stanford, would-be fledgling entrepreneurs had time to think and didn't have to worry about making payroll, increasing sales, or attending company meetings.

This notion of giving people the space they need, and even protecting that space, continues to prevail today.

"I definitely believe that downtime is productive time," says Evan Wittenberg, chief people officer at Box, which allows large companies to virtually store and share documents.

Evan, who looks freakishly young for someone who has been the director of Wharton's graduate leadership program, head of global leadership development at Google, and chief talent officer at HP, understands that downtime is often the missing complement to hard work. "The hard work you do is background for your downtime. Work your ass off and then when you're sitting under a tree is when the insight comes to you."

Box actively encourages downtime *during* the workday. It wouldn't be unusual to find someone playing a game on a Nintendo Wii or even going down a two-story slide at the company's Los Altos headquarters. "These are things that allow people to change their mode," Evan explains. "Changing your mode is so important to encourage innovative disruption. The downtime, the changing of context, is important. You'll see people at Box walking around the outside of a building talking to each other. They're having a meeting. They're changing their context from inside to outside, stale air to fresh air, artificial light to natural light."

Unusual Suspects in Silicon Valley

New companies, of course, need start-up capital in order to launch. One of the reasons young engineers back east couldn't imagine starting their own company fresh out of school was that no one would give them funding. They were, after all, young and by definition lacked a track record. But Terman wasn't the kind of guy who'd just throw his students into the deep end of the pool and expect them to swim.

He was able to use his government contacts to funnel money to his students' start-ups. In so doing, he introduced unusual suspects—young grads with fresh ideas and different perspectives—into the entrepreneurial world. At the same time, Terman introduced academics to the business world. Whereas professors used to stay in academic ivory towers, Terman encouraged them to sit on the boards of his students' new companies to serve as counselors and advisors.

In the valley, anyone could be an entrepreneur. It was within this culture that Robert Noyce, one of the eight dissatisfied engineers who left William Shockley's company to form Fairchild Semiconductor, went on to co-found Intel with Gordon Moore.

In his wonderful essay "Two Young Men Who Went West," Tom Wolfe traces Noyce's management style to his upbringing in the American tradition of dissenting

Protestantism known as Congregationalism. Growing up in a religion that emphasized a more communal form of leadership instilled in Noyce a looser management style, one that flattened hierarchies and valued input from all members of the company.

At Intel, Noyce allowed his young engineers a tremendous amount of freedom. As Wolfe put it, "Middle managers at Intel had more responsibility than most vice presidents back east." This faith in young employees, and the autonomy they were given, proved prescient in the early 1970s, when Ted Hoff, a young electrical engineer at Intel, invented the microprocessor. With the invention of the microprocessor, a new generation of independent young entrepreneurs began forming new companies, sometimes in their garages.

The same notion of bringing people into the fold continues to permeate the valley. "We want you to bring your wacky self to work every day," Evan Wittenberg told me, "because what that means is you're bringing your real self, your whole self. We need that. There is a benefit to bringing in different kinds of people to have them bounce off of each other. You don't get much wisdom from your crowd if everyone in your crowd is the same. We have varied clients, from WWF to P&G and Netflix; our different people help us understand our clients. I mean, the head of recruiting here is a world champion baton twirler. And I think that's a really good thing. We also have a member of the Higgs boson discovery team, a world champion juggler, two former professional cheerleaders, and a champion Go player. It's important that we have them all and that we let them share their ideas."

Terman's goal wasn't to create an entrepreneurial culture per se, but that is exactly what happened. A single individual set the standards and norms of Silicon Valley, which accelerated serendipity and created an innovative engine the likes of which have never been seen elsewhere.

Maintaining the culture is one of the best things a leader can do to encourage serendipity. At Box no one, including the CEO, has an office, so as to encourage people to circulate and meet one another. Employees can sit in on any meeting. Granted, this was easier two years ago when the company had thirty people and "everyone was in the soup." Today, with seven hundred employees, it is harder to maintain this culture of planned serendipity.

So one Tuesday each month, the company has what it calls "meet and eat." In the open lunchroom eight tables are covered with tablecloths. If you sit at one of them, you are signaling that you'd like to meet someone you don't know. Anyone is welcome to sit down with you, allowing you to strike up a conversation with someone in the company you have never met. The idea is not only to get employees to meet fellow employees but also to serve as a reminder to everyone at the company that they should be doing this more often.

Will Silicon Valley Lose Its Way?

"You have to remember that Frederick Terman had a purpose," Steve Blank said. "He was trying to help win the Cold War." As an illustration, Blank told me the story of his mentor, Bill Perry.

"He had a PhD in mathematics and is considered one of the fathers of stealth technology. He had been working at Sylvania and then left with eight other guys to start ESL [Electromagnetic Systems Laboratory]." Perry didn't leave because he thought he could make money; he left because he was trying to help the United States beat the Soviet Union in the Cold War. "He had decided that the best way to beat the Soviets was not to build better tanks. You can steal a tank and build your own and you're even. He concluded that the way to beat the Soviets was to out-engineer them. The way to win the Cold War was not to build tanks but to build semiconductors. The Soviets could steal all the semiconductors they wanted; they still couldn't make them."

Imagine an entrepreneur today starting a company for patriotic reasons. Indeed, the purpose that underlay Silicon Valley's culture fueled its productivity. After the end of the Cold War, however, the purpose shifted from responding to a crisis to making a profit. In other words, today's engineers are not necessarily working toward a higher purpose; most are looking to get rich. Blank believes this shift in values is already starting to erode the fabric Terman so assiduously wove.

After nearly sixty years of growth and innovation, the titans of Silicon Valley are no longer funded by the government. The money is coming from private venture capital firms looking for profit.

No longer are engineers looking to out-engineer the country's enemies; they are looking to out-IPO their neighbors. The arguable political ramifications of Facebook and Twitter for the Arab Spring were not the founding intentions of those social media companies but unintended consequences.

One of the great strengths of Silicon Valley has been the free flow of engineering talent from one company to another. In 2010, however, the Justice Department settled an antitrust case against Adobe, Google, Intuit, Intel, Pixar, and Apple for allegedly entering into a secret agreement not to hire one another's most desirable workers. "I believe we have a policy of no recruiting from Apple," Google's then-CEO wrote in a private email. A 2005 email described an agreement between Adobe's former CEO Bruce Chizen "not to solicit any Apple employees, and vice versa." On and on the emails go. The companies settled the case with the Justice Department without admitting guilt.

If top talent can't change jobs, then the sharing and movement of ideas will stop. Talented software engineers may stop being attracted to Silicon Valley. If that happens, the density of the network will erode and innovation will dim.

An offshoot of this culture of making money is the rise of "talent acquisition." Big companies with lots of money are buying small start-ups—not for their products or research but for the talented employees who work there. The innovative product may never come to market. The "talent" is absorbed into the larger organization, and innovation from below diminishes.

Yet, although Silicon Valley's innovation culture may be in danger, it continues to hum along, and no region has yet taken its place. Every few years we hear of some region that is building its own equivalent, but the would-be Silicon Valleys have never panned out. A centralized authority cannot simply will such a dynamic system into existence. Trying to legislate innovation demonstrates a fundamental misunderstanding of what makes Silicon Valley tick: the confluence of white space, renegades, and planned serendipity. Silicon Valley was not created by a decree from on high. It was encouraged by allowing the serendipitous clash and open exchange of ideas, with no preconceived plan for what might result.

(8)

THE FIVE RULES OF CHAOS

Every object in the room was filled with meaning and symbolism. There was the Civil War–era flag from the 2nd Armored Cavalry Regiment—"my first unit," General Dempsey said with pride as he showed me his office at the Pentagon. It had been three years since I first started working with the military, and I had come to respect and appreciate the institution's powerful relationship with American history. Across the wall was an oil painting of General George Marshall, creator of the Marshall Plan. "In my new job as chairman of the Joint Chiefs of Staff," reflected Dempsey, "I have to appreciate just how much Marshall did and how he was able to work across such a variety of different fields."

General Dempsey's desk was originally used by General Douglas MacArthur to plan the Pacific war during World War II.

If the objects in the large office were a chorus of history, one voice rose above the rest. Atop MacArthur's grand old desk, amid neatly arranged, color-coded folders and framed family portraits, sat a wooden box inscribed *Make It Matter*, the same box I'd seen on my first visit, which held cards representing each soldier who had been killed under Dempsey's command.

In one way or another, I had thought about that box every single day over the last few years. I felt I had come to know those men and women myself. I had met so many dedicated officers and soldiers just like them. I had had dinner with their families. I had seen where they lived and come to better understand why they joined the military to serve their country in the first place.

"There's danger out there," General Dempsey said of the current state of the world, "with the proliferation of weapons into the hands of those who previously didn't have access to them. You've got a changing relationship between the governed and the governing, and power is pulled from the center. All that creates chaos. We have a lot less control."

Whether you're the head of the U.S. armed forces or a manager of a corporate division, the temptation when encountering a chaotic situation is to crack down and try to instill as much order as possible. It's *very* tempting to try to structure chaos out of our lives and organizations. If you have a department that isn't productive enough, you enact stricter controls, impose check-ins and time lines, or work more closely with the individuals involved to make sure they're on track.

If we accept the premise that the world is getting more chaotic—from the Middle East to our local and global markets—we encounter an odd paradox. In attempting to keep chaos at bay, we risk squelching the very innovations and new ideas that will help advance our businesses and our futures.

I've argued in favor of bringing chaos into our organizational processes and decision making—and have worked with the military to do just that. But we shouldn't do so blindly, just hoping for the best. The key thing to understand from our journey is that while introducing chaos is inherently messy, there are also rules for managing it. The five rules I suggest below apply across groups and organizations, whether you're trying to change a multimillion-member organization like the military, attempting to transform a start-up company, or hoping to make a difference in a school system.

Rule 1: Avoid the Seductive Lure of Data and Measurements

"If you were to look at it by the numbers," Steve Rotkoff told me one day, "it looked like the United States was going to easily conquer Iraq."

"So much for those numbers," I said, considering how difficult bringing peace to Iraq proved to be. Had the military botched its analysis?

"It's not necessarily that the numbers were imprecise. It's that we tried to apply precision to a situation that was imprecise." He went on to explain that the problem was endemic: "Senior leaders must quickly make lots of important up or down decisions. Toward these ends, we train decision makers to evaluate the data. But the problem is that often, in order to make the *right* decision, we need not just data but the narrative that explains the situation. The thing is that narrative takes time; data does not." And so in the service of precision, critical facts that couldn't be represented as numerical data were ignored, and the consequences were dire.

Over the years I've come to see how much truth there is in the army adage "If you can't measure it, then it doesn't exist." One example that comes to mind arose from the work I was doing with one of the army's schools.

During my program, individuals shared stories about

overseas battles, dealing with fellow soldiers dying in combat, and their hope that they might be able to use contained chaos to become better leaders. Groups discussed how to bring more voices into the conversation, how to create white space in their days, and how to increase communication among disparate parts of the army.

The feedback from the program was overwhelmingly positive. One officer wrote in his evaluation that the circle sessions were "unlike any leadership program I have been exposed to in twelve years of service. It was more valuable than any of four combat deployments." Another officer said the program was "the most significant opportunity to reflect and build self-awareness I have ever experienced." Yet another wrote about his family and the program's effect on his "spirituality, my marriage, my role as a father, and my own self-view. My hope is that the experience does not end with me."

Raving quotes are one thing, but numbers are another. When surveyed months after the program, 90 percent of participants were able to describe at least one significant example of something they had already done differently as a result of having gone through the program; an equal percentage were able to cite at least one significant example of an instance when they were able to achieve a better outcome through incorporating what they had learned.

But such anecdotal evidence was still too imprecise for the army school. Though extremely positive, the feedback was difficult to plug into a standard army matrix. It's hard to objectively evaluate statements about becoming better leaders or more innovative problem solvers.

The army wanted a *precise measurement* of the impact of my program on its graduates. Although done with the best of intentions, what happened next was almost comical. Several months after they completed my program, my officers were continuing their studies at another army school. During one class session, school administrators sent in an evaluator armed with a checklist and a pen.

The evaluator took copious notes on how many times my officers raised their hands and compared that number to how many times students who *hadn't* gone through the program raised their hands. Remember, the men and women being evaluated were accomplished officers—most of them had led troops into battle. The assumption however, was that improved leadership, stronger engagement, and greater adaptability could be measured by how many times individuals raised their hands.

The hand-raising survey was an attempt at imposing precision into the chaos equation—but it also completely missed the point. "What I learned in the program was to listen and to create white space by being quiet," one officer told me, shaking his head with frustration.

He added wryly, "If bringing in chaos into the army is going to be evaluated by how many times we *raise our hands*, then the army should have just purchased elbow rests, and we can raise our hands all day long."

By its very nature, organized chaos is imprecise. Without meaning to, organizations continue to conduct the equivalent of the hand-raising test. Trying to apply precision by measuring results (e.g., your default mode network should provide you with 3.8 insights a day) obscures the role of contained chaos in a structured organization and fails to recognize the subtlety and nuance of the process.

Rule 2: Remember, It's Called Organized Chaos

"What we do here," said Cort Worthington, the UC Berkeley professor who ran the army circle sessions with me, "is like driving a truck downhill on a road."

"A curvy, icy, *mountain* road," I added.

"Yeah, and the brakes don't quite work." He started to laugh.

"And the steering is a little loose."

Managing a chaotic process is a trying experience if you're fond of control. It's hard to imagine, for example, exhibiting Professor Joe Neilands's patience with Kary

Mullis and his hijinks at the biochemistry labs in our own workplaces. I still get inspired when I think of Joe telling me about the "field of a thousand flowers." That said, there's a flip side to the coin. We can't ignore the fact that Mullis did his research inside a very *structured* environment, with protocols, university budgets, and, yes, a bureaucracy. Joe's role was two-sided. He both fostered chaos *and* contained it. He kept the university at arm's length with regard to Mullis's research, but he also kept Mullis on task, doing the work he needed to do. And of course Joe recognized that Mullis was brilliant—it was worth giving this unusual, and unusually talented, suspect some free rein. It wasn't as if Joe opened the doors to his lab to anyone who walked in off the street.

Similarly, Nintendo CEO Hiroshi Yamauchi protected Shigeru Miyamoto and gave him the freedom to design something new. But Miyamoto never would have been able to bring Donkey Kong to life had it not been for the structure the company provided. The CEO created a pocket of chaos and protected it, while ensuring that the rest of the company was well managed.

The Stanford Graduate School of Business fosters serendipity, but any student will tell you that there are also required courses and an enormously challenging and full curriculum. The serendipity takes place *within* this structured environment.

And I would not have been successful bringing

organized chaos into the military were it not for its structure. "We are hierarchical," explained General Dempsey, "but the truth is that warfare has become a lot less hierarchical and more chaotic."

The last time I spoke with Dempsey was during the early months of 2013, amid the difficult budget uncertainty that came with sequestration. "The budget uncertainty, frankly, makes it extraordinarily hard to bring in chaos. Any corporate leader would need the same thing I need. We're trying to introduce chaos in the face of uncertainty. It's funny," he continued, "because I need certainty in order to make the kind of changes [introducing chaos] that we're talking about."

Therein lies the paradox of the first two rules. We need leaders who can tolerate uncertainty and imprecision, but we also need leaders who can maintain stability *around* the chaos.

Rule 3: Make White Space Productive

Here are four concrete ways to create, sustain, and utilize white space:

1. Employ white space judiciously.

Remember that white space is particularly useful when you've already devoted a significant amount of mental energy to a project and have a clear goal in mind. Frank Gehry, for example, grappled with his skyscraper dilemma for months, and his goal was clear: to give his building a feeling of movement.

That's why the army circles were so productive. Officers are trained to be efficient and hardworking. Before coming to my program, they'd spent years in their jobs, thinking about a host of complex issues. The white space I provided, with the explicit goal of making the army more adaptive, allowed them time to synthesize and integrate their myriad experiences.

A slacker whiling away his days has plenty of time to daydream but doesn't necessarily benefit from white space. But ironically, a team working against a deadline— with seemingly no time to spare—can benefit from staring into space or even taking an entire day off to reflect.

So take a walk or allow yourself to daydream when you've reached an impasse in tackling the problem you're working on. Give your team time and space to reflect when they've been working nonstop on a project.

2. Consider how much is too much.

There is no magical answer about how much white space an organization should provide.

Rather than try to guess, why not ask the people who

work with you? Ask, "Do you feel like you have time to brainstorm and think about new ways of doing things? Or do you feel you spend all of your time putting out fires and handling routine day-to-day tasks?"

When I work with army officers, I continually ask them about the level of structure they feel they need. Surprisingly, there have been plenty of times when they told me they wanted *less* unstructured time.

3. Move!

Just as sitting back in our chairs and staring into space gives our brains time to power up the default mode network, so does exercise, especially the kind that doesn't require intense focus (such as using a StairMaster or treadmill or riding a stationary bike).

A study led by Dr. Jim McKenna at Leeds Metropolitan University in England sought to evaluate the effect of exercise on work. The results showed that 65 percent of employees exhibited improved time management, productivity, and interpersonal performance on days that they exercised.

4. Create a micro white space.

I've learned an especially useful technique from Lisa Kimball about creating white space in a meeting, regardless of the size of the group and length of the meeting.

Most of us would describe a successful meeting as one where participants are fully engaged and fire off ideas one after another.

We're almost allergic to awkward silences. Because of that, when we ask a question, we give participants only a second or two before calling on someone or simply moving on.

But when Lisa asks a question, to give participants more time for ideas to gel, she silently counts to twenty—slowly. "I make sure to not look anybody in the eyes," she explained, "because it creates pressure, so instead I look down at my shoes." Surprisingly, it results in more and better ideas. "Silly as it sounds, countless times someone chimes in as I'm reaching eighteen or nineteen in my count."

Along similar lines, try this: before starting a discussion, ask everyone to spend a minute thinking about ideas in silence. It can be a surprising way to spark new ideas. In fact, it's amazing how often someone will interrupt the silence before the time is up. I let the group know from the outset that while it might be uncomfortable, we're going to keep to a minute of silence. "It's the first time," one participant told me, "that I've actually reflected on an idea before shouting it out. What a difference sixty seconds make!"

Rule 4: Embrace Unusual Suspects

"What I've observed over time," General Dempsey said when I spoke to him last, "is that if I don't *deliberately* try to learn, then not only will I fail to advance, but I'll actually fall backwards." What's true for General Dempsey, I believe, is true for today's organizations as well.

When we hire or recruit someone to a team, we tend to be drawn to those individuals who are similar to us. As my brother, Rom, and I explained in *Click*, having something in common with people—even if it's something as meaningless as sharing the same name or birthday—makes us like them and trust them more and encourages us to be more helpful to them.

There's so much psychologically that pushes us to reach out to people who are similar to us in our thinking, behavior, background, and interests that we need to actively seek out the unusual suspect. In doing so, ask yourself the following questions.

1. Is this person really unusual?

Being younger or older or having a different racial or religious background doesn't necessarily mean that the person is an unusual suspect. Such a person may still approach organizational, technological, or operational problems with the same old set of assumptions and solutions.

Moreover, who is and who is not an unusual suspect can shift depending on the context. Nate Silver was an unusual suspect in the world of political polling but wouldn't have been one in the world of sports statistics. Here's one rule of thumb: is the person someone you would not otherwise have interacted with? Of course, that can create a temptation to go to the other extreme, which leads to the next question.

2. Are you confusing unusual with crazy?

Consider the story of Dr. William Minor, a surgeon by training who spent the second half of his life as a man of letters. The doctor received frequent shipments of books, and as he read them in his teak-lined library, he kept meticulous notes indexing specific words and their usage.

In the late nineteenth century, the *Oxford English Dictionary (OED)* set out on the ambitious task of providing examples of each word's usage in books and plays. Its staff asked avid readers for help, and Dr. Minor was up for the task.

The first word he was given was *art*. Consulting his index, Minor readily found examples going back to the 1500s. To the *OED* scholars, overworked, underpaid, and relying on an inferior indexing system, Dr. Minor was a gift from heaven. Whenever they found themselves stuck on a word, Dr. Minor came to the rescue, eventually providing upward of twelve thousand examples, more than any other outside contributor. Fast and accurate, he soon became an irreplaceable part of the *OED* team.

The thing that you need to know about Dr. Minor, though, was that his teak-lined library room was situated inside block 2 of the Broadmoor Criminal Lunatic Asylum. He'd been incarcerated for killing an unarmed man in cold blood. Some speculate that he suffered from post-traumatic stress disorder. Others pointed to signs of schizophrenia.

Sure, the *OED* benefited from Dr. Minor's work. But not many of us would want to work with such an individual in the next cubicle.

Ask yourself whether a would-be unusual suspect could get along with others in your group or organization, or whether he or she would be impossibly disruptive. Can this person tolerate some level of management and supervision, or is he or she completely unable to function within a hierarchy? Is this a person you wouldn't otherwise encounter—or an individual you'd go out of your way to avoid?

3. Are you missing an unusual suspect who is already inside the organization?

Remember Lisa Kimball's smorgasbord groups in the hospitals? Whenever she facilitates a group and someone says something like "they" or "those people," she immediately stops the conversation. Doing so is not a lesson in political correctness; it's about finding unusual suspects.

"Once we talk about someone from a different department," explains Lisa, "it means that we're talking about someone who needs to be involved in the conversation." After stopping the conversation, Lisa will contact the would-be unusual suspect and invite him or her to the next meeting or even take the entire group over to the person's office.

When people who are not in the group are mentioned or come up, it means that they're in some way relevant to the conversation. The fact that they're not in the room might be a clue that they are unusual suspects in the context of this group (i.e., people with whom we wouldn't normally interact, at least not within this group). Inviting new people to the table—from different departments or disciplines and from different levels of the company's or organization's hierarchy—can help open the door for serendipity.

Rule 5: Organize Serendipity

While organized or planned serendipity might seem like the most amorphous of the concepts in this book, it is also the easiest to implement—you just have to set the conditions to encourage people to have spontaneous interactions. Remember, planned serendipity isn't about waiting to get lucky.

In order to cut through bureaucratic red tape and increase collaboration among government employees, the Dutch government created a variety of initiatives, including an online reservation system called Deelstoel, which translates as "share chair." Each government office sets aside a portion of its building for use by other government organizations. All an individual or group needs to do is to log in and make a reservation online, the same way you'd reserve a conference room at work.

Employees sign up to use the available office space for different reasons. One person uses it to work a few minutes from home, rather than driving sixty miles to and from work every day. Another simply enjoys working from different locations in her city throughout the week. The benefit to the Dutch government is in encouraging people from different departments to bring their expertise and ideas into offices that otherwise would never be exposed to them.

It's a theme that can't be overemphasized. The goal in encouraging serendipity is to create openness, encourage the flow of new ideas, and allow people to bump into one another. Imagine the possibilities that might result from these kinds of spontaneous collisions.

When I was in his office recently, I asked General Dempsey to reflect about his decision to conduct the chaos experiment with me. In the past few years, hundreds of individuals—from sergeants to generals—have gone through my program. Was it a useful exercise? After several seconds of thoughtful silence, he replied, "We don't have any choice, actually. This isn't a cute idea— 'Wouldn't it be cute to see how leaders react to chaos?' It's about effectively responding to this new world we live in." I couldn't agree more. The ground is shifting under our feet constantly, whether we work for the government or some hot new Silicon Valley start-up, whether we work in the energy business or the service industry. In order to make our organizations more nimble, resilient, responsive, and innovative—in order to *survive*—we have to accept chaos into our lives, even invite it.

Acknowledgments

ORI BRAFMAN:

It's only appropriate that a book about chaos would have its share of, well, chaos. It was written on military bases late at night, in cafés across San Francisco, and in New York apartments involving treasure chests of jewelry and the Secret Service. I'm indebted to everyone who's made this entire journey possible.

Judah Pollack has been a partner involved in every bit of the writing process through thick and thin since the book's inception, and I'm fortunate to have benefited from his unrelenting curiosity, his tireless dedication, and his creative mind, which is an extraordinary incubator for ideas. Rom Brafman, as always, prevented the process from becoming overly chaotic and is the most supportive and selfless brother anyone could hope for. Kelly McVicker was an instrumental part of the writing and editing process and encouraged, inspired, and offered bits of magic when I needed them most. Steve Rotkoff's insights into the army were invaluable, and

I'm grateful to have had him as a friend through this process. Hilary Roberts and her red pencil continue to make me sound more refined—not an easy feat. I appreciate the discerning eyes of Alison Roberts, Heather Gunther, and Lori Matheson, who lent their time to read the manuscript at various stages along the way.

I'm fortunate to have gotten to know General Martin Dempsey. His leadership gives even a Berkeley person like me faith in the military. Dave Horan has been a trusted guide and has offered enormously helpful advice. Maxie McFarland and Greg Fontenot were key in bringing my program to the army. I'm continually grateful to the soldiers and officers who participated in the program, as well as the soldiers and families across the nation who continue to serve.

Esther Newberg and her team at ICM—Liz Farrell, Kari Stuart, and Zoe Sandler—continue to be unwavering champions. I can't imagine a better team to have on my side. Similarly, Roger Scholl has been a creative ally and gracious editor. His team at Random House—publisher Tina Constable, editor in chief Mauro DiPreta, publicity and marketing director Tara Gilbride, publicist Ayelet Gruenspecht, production editor Cindy Berman, editorial assistant Derek Reed, interior book designer Songhee Kim, and jacket designer Drue Dixon—have been a joy to work with.

Throughout the writing process, I've been bolstered

by the support of family and friends: Tsilla and Hagay Brafman, Nira Chaikin, Josyn Herce, Megan and John Hutchinson, Lisa Kimball, Cort Worthington, Ron Ricci, Chip Colbert, Jason Thomas, Matt Brady, Denise Egri, Amy Pospiech, Dina Kaplan, Noah Kagan, Matt Miller and Katie Brown, David Blatte, Corey Modeste, Aviva Mohilner, Jessica Laughlin, Liz O'Donnell, Sara Olsen, Josh Rosenblum, Mark Schlosberg, Michael Breyer, Amy Shuster, Rachman Blake, Pete Sims, Rudy Tan, Pam and Roy Webb, Kimberly Wicoff, Melanie Yelton, Barrett Horne, Ron Martin, and so many others. I'm fortunate to have you in my life.

JUDAH POLLACK:

First I must thank Ori Brafman, for asking me what I was working on, for then inviting me on this trip, and for captaining the ship through storms and doldrums. To my formal guides, Rosenberg, Benjy, Isa, Cort, Lisa. And to my informal ones, Allan, Barrett, Olivia. To my ladies of genius, Sera and Meg, for letting me sit in. And to those patient souls, otherwise known as my family, for listening: Darci, Kate, Dov, Michael, Debarati, Noah, Hugh, Mom, and Dad. And to Tara, for loving me.

NOTES

INTRODUCTION: THE BOTTOM LINE

ix Ron Ricci at Cisco Systems: Information from Ron Ricci comes from a series of interviews conducted by the authors with Ricci from September to November 2010.

CHAPTER 1: HARNESSING CHAOS

7 The death toll wasn't measured: Peter Gay and R. K. Webb, *Modern Europe to 1815* (1973), 52; Walter S. Zapotoczny, "The Political and Social Consequences of the Black Death, 1348–1351" (2006), www .wzaponline.com/BlackDeath.pdf, 2; Jack Weatherford, *Genghis Khan and the Making of the Modern World* (2004), 245.

7 London lost 40 percent: David Herlihy, *The Black Death and the Transformation of the West* (1997), 17.

7 The Black Death arrived: Ibid., 51.

7 When the plague arrived: Weatherford, 158–59.

8 The plague entered Britain: Norman F. Cantor, *In the Wake of the Plague* (2001), 11–12.

8 Rats were a common sight: Ibid., 21.

8 As it scurried through Bristol: Bristol Link, "The History of Bristol," www.Bristol-link.co.uk/history.

9 It was this busy world: Cantor, 21–22.

9 At first there would have been no discernible change: Herlihy, 22.

10 Instead, it brought about: Charles Van Doren, A *History of Knowledge* (1992).

12 Here is an example: Gay and Webb, 64.

12 At the time, the Bible was: Ibid., 20.

13 Boccaccio was of a different breed: Ibid., 60–69.

13 At the time of the plague: Herlihy, 60–70.

15 In fact, the humanists poured: Cantor, 206–7.

15 In other words: Weatherford, 245.

16 In 1419 Florence held a competition: Ross King, *Brunelleschi's Dome: How a Renaissance Genius Reinvented Architecture* (2001).

17 At the same time, another young man: James Hitchcock, *History of the Catholic Church: From the Apostolic Age to the Third Millennium* (2012), 243.

17 With this shift: Ruth Tenzler Feldman, *The Fall of Constantinople (Pivotal Moments in History)* (2007), 74.

18 Traditionally, books had been copied: Herlihy, 49–50.

19 At the same time: Van Doren.

22 Of the 250,000 types of seeds: W. P. Armstrong, "Drift Seeds and Drift Fruits," waynesword.palomar.edu/pldec398.htm.

24 In fact, nature loves: Forest Encyclopedia Network, "Fire Effects on Soil Nutrients," www.forestencyclopedia.net/p/p679.

25 Sixty-five million years ago: Katherine Harmon, "A Theory Set in Stone: An Asteroid Killed the Dinosaurs

After All," *Scientific American*, March 4, 2010, www
.scientificamerican.com/article.cfm?id=asteroid-killed
-dinosaurs.

27 But on Sundays, Rotkoff and a small group: Based on
interviews with Ret. Col. Steve Rotkoff from 2010 to
2013.

CHAPTER 2: CONTAINED CHAOS

32 Take, for example, Yaron: Ivars Peterson, "Trouble
with Wild Card Poker," http://mathtourist.blogspot
.com/2009/02/trouble-with-wild-card-poker.html;
Presh Talwalkar, "Wild Card Poker Paradox," http://
mindyourdecisions.com/blog/2010/05/25/wild-card
-poker-paradox.

34 If you had visited: Jason Fried, "Why I Gave My Company a Month Off," *Inc.*, August 22, 2012, www.inc
.com/magazine/201209/jason-fried/why-company
-a-month-off.html; Jessica Stillman, "Slow Business: The Case Against Fast Growth," *Inc.*, September 18, 2012, http://www.inc.com/jessica-stillman/slow
-business-fast-growth-is-not-good-for-the-company
.html.

36 "We don't 'predict'": John Reinan, "Why Gallup
Hates Nate Silver," *Minnpost*, November 19, 2012,
http://www.minnpost.com/business/2012/11/why
-gallup-hates-nate-silver.

37 Silver spent six years: Peter Keating, "Predicting the
Future," *ESPN Magazine*, December 4, 2012.

39 Lisa Kimball doesn't look: All stories about liberating
structures and combating the spread of staph infection
in hospitals come from interviews with Lisa Kimball
between 2010 and 2012.

CHAPTER 3: EINSTEIN'S BRAIN

45 Letters started pouring in: Dennis Overbye, *Einstein in Love: A Scientific Romance* (2000), 147.

46 When Einstein died: Jon Hamilton, "Einstein's Brain Unlocks Some Mysteries of the Mind," *Morning Edition*, NPR, June 2, 2010.

47 Scientists found that: Dustin Grinnell, "What's So Special About Einstein's Brain," *Eureka*, May 7, 2012, http://crivereureka.com/einsteins-brain.

47 Another scientist: Marian Diamond, "On the Brain of a Scientist: Albert Einstein," *Experimental Neurology*, April 1985, www.ncbi.nlm.nih.gov/pubmed/3979509; Dr. David Dubin, "Glia: The Cinderella of Brain Cells," Akashia Center for Integrative Medicine, www.akashacenter.com/resources/articles/glia-the-cinderella-of-brain-cells; N. Heins, "Glial Cells Generate Neurons: The Role of the Transcription Factor Pax6," *Nature Neuroscience*, April 2002, www.ncbi.nlm.nih.gov/pubmed/11896398.

49 At the University of Zurich: Overbye, 19–27.

49 In the summer: Ibid., 49.

49 He couldn't be bothered: Ibid., 62.

52 And yet, as research by Dr. Marcus Raichle: Marcus Raichle, "The Brain's Dark Energy," *Scientific American*, March 2010, 44–49; Stephen Wiedner, "Interview with UCSB Psychology Professor Jonathan Schooler," *Noomii*, April 17, 2009, www.noomii.com/blog/174-interview-with-meta-awareness-professor-jonathan-schooler.

57 A few weeks after my meeting: From work done at the CGSC and interviews with Ret. Col. Steve Rotkoff.

59 In the 1960s, as part of his war on poverty: Office of Superintendent of Public Instruction, "Elementary and Secondary Education Act," www.k12.wa.us/esea; U.S. Department of Education, "Title I—Improving

the Academic Achievement of the Disadvantaged," www2.ed.gov/policy/elsec/leg/esea02/pg1.html.

59 Although the program was a complete failure: National Commission on Excellence in Education, *A Nation at Risk: The Imperative for Educational Reform* (1983); Margaret A. Jorgensen and Jenny Hoffmann, "History of the No Child Left Behind Act of 2001 (NCLB)," Person Assessment Report, 2003.

60 Over the next ten years: U.S. Department of Education, *Federal Education Policy and the States, 1945–2009*, www.archives.nysed.gov/edpolicy/research/res_essay _bush_ghw_busn_achvmt.shtml.

61 New standards were set: "No Child Left Behind," *Education Week*, updated September 19, 2011, www.edweek.org/ew/issues/no-child-left-behind; Brian Resnick, "The Mess of No Child Left Behind," *Atlantic Monthly*, December 16, 2011.

61 But an unintended consequence: Gordon Cawelti, "The Side Effects of NCLB," *Educational Leadership* 64, no. 3 (2006): 64–68.

62 Surely all this has led: "No Child Left Behind," *Education Week*; William J. Bennett, "U.S. Lag in Science, Math a Disaster in the Making," CNN.com, February 9, 2012, www.cnn.com/2012/02/09/opinion/ bennett-stem-education.

62 When we look at countries: "Best Education in the World: Finland, South Korea Top Country Rankings, U.S. Rated Average," *Huffington Post*, November 27, 2012, http://www.huffingtonpost.com/2012/11/27/best -education-in-the-wor_n_2199795.html.

62 But the other difference: Harry Wray, *Japanese and American Education: Attitudes and Practices* (1999), 255–59.

63 Einstein barely completed: Overbye, 91.

63 His situation was similar to: Ken Burns, *Thomas Jefferson*, PBS, 2000.

64 When he submitted his dissertation: Overbye, 91.

64 Einstein created his own rag-tag team: Overbye, 109–12.

66 In 2009, researchers at the Albert Einstein College of Medicine: Romina M. Barros, Ellen J. Silver, and Ruth E. K. Sten, "School Recess and Group Classroom Behavior," *Pediatrics*, February 1, 2009.

67 The reasoning behind this trend: Anthony D. Pellegrini, "Preschool and Primary School Education: Give Children a Break," *Jakarta Post*, March 28, 2005.

69 Anthony Pellegrini and Catherine Bohn: Anthony Pellegrini and Catherine Bohn, "The Role of Recess in Children's Cognitive Performance and School Adjustment," *Research News and Comment*, January/February 2005.

70 Asian students are given this type: Harold W. Stevenson, "Learning from Asian Schools," *Scientific American*, December 1992.

71 These recess studies have dramatic implications: Joe Verghese, "Leisure Activities and the Risk of Dementia in the Elderly," *New England Journal of Medicine*, June 2003.

71 Could it be the sociability of dancing: Richard Powers, "Use It or Lose It: Dancing Makes You Smarter," Stanford University, July 30, 2010, http://socialdance .stanford.edu/syllabi/smarter.htm.

73 In 1903 most of Einstein's Olympia Academy: Overbye, 112.

74 Here is how journalist Dennis Overbye: Ibid., 121.

74 So what did Einstein actually see: Ibid., 124–40; Peter Galison, *Einstein's Clocks, Poincaré's Maps* (2003), 14–26, 243–63.

76 Two years later, still working: Overbye, 150.

CHAPTER 4: THE NEUROBIOLOGY OF INSIGHT

84 It was to be architect Frank Gehry's: Paul Goldberger, "Gracious Living," *New Yorker*, March 7, 2011.

87 In a way, Gehry was in a predicament similar: Paul Strathern, *Medeleyev's Dream: The Quest for the Elements* (2002).

89 Scientists discovered that when a subject: Raichle; Michael D. Greicius, "Functional Connectivity in the Resting Brain: A Network Analysis of the Default Mode Hypothesis," *PNAS*, August 21, 2002, 253–58.

92 Dr. Raichle noticed a second clue: Greicius.

92 But there was a third clue: Raichle.

94 In fact, the network is always on: Greicius; Raichle.

94 To answer this question: Raichle.

95 That is, our brain has an internal story: Debra A. Gusnard, "Medial Prefrontal Cortex and Self-Referential Mental Activity: Relation to a Default Mode of Brain Function," *PNAS*, March 20, 2001.

95 This ratio—between the amount of energy: John M. Pearson, "Neurons in Posterior Cingulate Cortex Signal Exploratory Decisions in a Dynamic Multioption Choice Task," *Current Biology*, September 2009; John M. Pearson, "Posterior Cingulate Cortex: Adapting Behavior to a Changing World," *Trends in Cognitive Sciences*, April 2011; Mandana Modirrousta and Lesley K. Fellows, "Dorsal Medial Prefrontal Cortex Plays a Necessary Role in Rapid Error Prediction in Humans," *Journal of Neuroscience*, December 17, 2008.

96 Our brains construct these narratives: Gusnard; Yvette L. Sheline, "The Default Mode Network and Self-Referential Processes in Depression," *PNAS*, December 2008; interview with Yvette L. Sheline, "Yvette Sheline on the Default Mode Network and Depression," YouTube, December 2010.

97 Take the French novelist Marcel Proust: Marcel

Proust, *Remembrance of Things Past* (Wordsworth Editions, 2006).

98 To understand the power: Pearson.

99 Another hub of the default mode network: Peter Fransson and Guillaume Marrelec, "The Precuneus/Posterior Cingulate Cortex Plays a Pivotal Role in the Default Mode Network: Evidence from a Partial Correlation Network Analysis," *NeuroImage*, September 2008.

100 Gehry was staying up late: Goldberger.

100 Gehry had first seen the statue: Jackie Cooperman, "Frank Gehry: A Sit-Down with the Artist of Architecture," *Wall Street Journal*, April 2, 2011.

101 Bernini's sculpture sits: Marcelle Auclair, *Saint Teresa of Avila* (1953).

102 In the mid-1960s Gary Starkweather: Charlene O'Hanlon, "Gary Starkweather—Laser Printer Inventor," CRN News, November 13, 2002.

103 After staying awake for three nights: Strathern.

104 Einstein experienced a similar eureka moment: Overbye, 135.

105 Back when Google was still a start-up: Stephen Levy, *In the Plex: How Google Thinks, Works, and Shapes Our Lives* (2011), 95–125.

107 J. K. Rowling has described: J. K. Rowling, "Biography," *JKRowling.com*.

CHAPTER 5: SURFING NAKED

123 PCR is the genetic equivalent: "PCR: Introduction," National Center for Biotechnology Information, NIH, www.ncbi.nim.nih.gov; "Polymerase Chain Reaction (PCR)," YouTube, March 2010.

124 Here is how Mullis explained the process: Kary Mullis, "Nobel Lecture," December 8, 1993.

127 I'm sure that, had she met him: David Sheff, *Game*

Over: How Nintendo Zapped an American Industry, Captured Your Dollars, and Enslaved Your Children (1993), 3–56.

132 "What if you walk along": Quoted ibid., 37.

134 That is exactly what happened: Jervis Anderson, *This Was Harlem* (1981), 236, 240, 310; Marshall and Jean Stearns, *Jazz Dance* (1994), 110–11, 201–2; Ken Burns, *Jazz*, episodes 2 and 4, PBS, 2000.

135 Born in Chicago in 1909: Anderson, 309–13; Stearns, 296, 317, 324, 328; Burns, *Jazz*, episodes 3–5.

137 Cardinal Nicholas of Cusa, for example: "Nicholas of Cusa," *Catholic Encyclopedia*, www.newadvent.org.

138 At Cisco Systems, Ron Ricci: Ron Ricci, from a series of interviews conducted by the authors with Ricci from September to November 2010.

140 Coming out of retirement to become: Interviews with Steve Rotkoff and Kevin Benson, Red Team University, UFMCS, U.S. Army.

CHAPTER 6: ACCELERATING SERENDIPITY

149 Marie Mookini was easily the person: From an interview the writers conducted with Marie Mookini on September 26, 2012.

150 "About 50 to 60 percent of the class": From an interview the writers conducted with Allison Rouse on September 28, 2012.

156 Robin Starbuck Farmanfarmaian: From an interview the writers conducted with Robin Starbuck Farmanfarmaian on October 14, 2012.

159 It was the kind of gathering: William D. Cohan, "Huffing and Puffing," *Vanity Fair*, February 2011.

160 Eighteenth-century salons: From an interview with Debarati Sanyal, professor of modern French at UC Berkeley, October 2, 2012.

161 Seven decades earlier, in the 1930s: Anne-Marie

O'Connor, "Reviving Salons as Hotbeds of New Ideas," *Los Angeles Times*, January 24, 2001.

167 The results were surprising: Giam Sweigers, "Talking Business: Giam Swiegers, CEO Deloitte Australia— RMIT University," YouTube, April 28, 2011.

168 In response, some companies have turned to: Lawrence W. Cheek, "In New Office Designs, Room to Roam and to Think," *New York Times*, March 17, 2012; John Tierney, "From Cubicles, Cry for Quiet Pierces Office Buzz," *New York Times*, May 19, 2012.

169 This is why New York mayor Michael Bloomberg: Chris Smith, "Open City," *New York*, September 26, 2010.

170 Ed Skyler, the deputy mayor for administration: Anthony Ramirez, "Mimicking Bloomberg's Bullpen, with Extra Spice," *New York Times*, April 15, 2006.

171 Washington, D.C.'s former mayor, Adrian Fenty: Christopher Swope, "Warming Up in the Bullpen," *Governing*, February 22, 2007, http://www.governing.com/blogs/view/Warming-Up-in-the.html.

171 The bullpen allows for a greater flow: Michael Bloomberg, *Bloomberg by Bloomberg* (1997).

CHAPTER 7: PUTTING IT ALL TOGETHER

172 Being in Robert Swanson's shoes: Genentech, "Our Founders," gene.com; Leslie Pray, "Recombinant DNA Technology and Transgenic Animals," nature.com/scitable, 2008.

173 Robert Swanson, meanwhile: Interview with Herbert Boyer, DNA Learning Center, dnalc.org.

174 Saxenian's first theory involves: AnnaLee Saxenian, *Regional Advantage: Culture and Competition in Silicon Valley and Route 128* (1996); AnnaLee Saxenian, "Silicon Valley vs. Route 128," *Inc.*, February 1, 1994.

175 Entrepreneur Frank Levinson: Gregory Gomorov, "Silicon Valley History," netvalley.com, citing Frank

Levinson, A *Tale of Lambs, Preschoolers, and Networking* (2001).

175 AnnaLee Saxenian's second theory: Saxenian, *Regional Advantage*.

176 William Shockley, the co-inventor of the transistor: "Bill Shockley: Part I," pbs.org, courtesy of the American Institute of Physics; Tom Wolfe, "Two Young Men Who Went West," *Hooking Up* (2000), 17–65; Gomorov.

178 Fairchild Semiconductor got its name: Arthur Rock, "Done Deals: Venture Capitalists Tell Their Story: Featured HBS Arthur Rock," Harvard Business School Working Knowledge series, www.hbswk.hbs.edu, December 4, 2000.

179 The psychologist took a professorship: Carolyn E. Tajnai, "Fred Terman, the Father of Silicon Valley," Stanford Computer Forum, May 1985, www.siliconvalley -usa.com/about/terman.html; interview with Professor Steven Blank, May 2011.

181 It all began with the military: Interview with Blank.

185 While still at Stanford: Interview with Evan Wittenberg, January 2012.

187 In his wonderful essay: Wolfe.

188 The same notion of bringing people: Interview with Wittenberg.

190 "You have to remember": Interview with Blank.

191 One of the great strengths of Silicon Valley: Dan Gillmor, "Collusion in Silicon Valley: How High Does It Go?" Salon.com, September 27, 2010.

192 An offshoot of this culture: Dan Bobkoff, "Employee Shopping: Acqui-Hire Is the New Normal in Silicon Valley, All Tech Considered," NPR.org, September 24, 2012.

Index

10/13